SAN MATEO CITY PUBLIC LIBRARY

D0621925

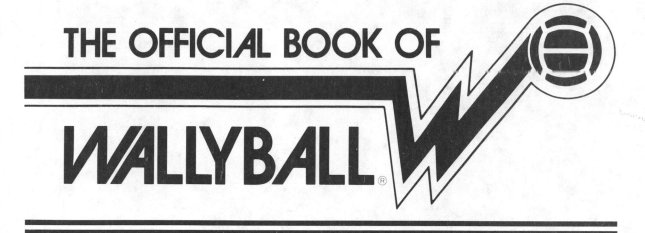

THE OFFICIAL BOOK OF WALLYBALL.

JOE GARCIA
CREATOR OF WALLYBALL.
WITH MURRAY DUBIN

CONTEMPORARY
BOOKS, INC.
CHICAGO ▪ NEW YORK

Public Library San Mateo, CA

Library of Congress Cataloging-in-Publication Data

Garcia, Joe.
   The official book of wallyball.

   1. Wallyball.   I. Title.
GV1017.W34G37   1986   796.32'5   86-4378
ISBN 0-8092-5080-2

796.32⁵
GAR

Wallyball is the owner of the trademark "WALLYBALL" used in conjunction with the games whose rules are contained in this book. The name Wallyball may not be used in connection with this game, tournaments thereof, or sports garments bearing the name Wallyball without the express written permission of Wallyball.

Inquiries regarding licensing arrangements for the use of the trademark Wallyball should be directed to Wallyball International, Inc.; 11050 Santa Monica Boulevard; Los Angeles, California 90025

All photos by Rick Stewart, Focus West

Copyright © 1986 by Joe Garcia
All rights reserved
Published by Contemporary Books, Inc.
180 North Michigan Avenue, Chicago, Illinois 60601
Manufactured in the United States of America
Library of Congress Catalog Card Number: 86-4378
International Standard Book Number: 0-8092-5080-2

Published simultaneously in Canada by Beaverbooks, Ltd.
195 Allstate Parkway, Valleywood Business Park
Markham, Ontario L3R 4T8 Canada

To my parents, Lydia and Cesar, who taught me persistence and sensitivity; I love you more than I'll ever be able to show you. To my brother, Jimmy, who has always been there when I needed him. To P.J., the best thing that has ever happened to me. To Kevin Doyle, the best friend a man could ever hope to have. To Jim Perrine, for supporting me when I needed it most. To Michael O'Hara and Paul Sunderland, for being my partners and friends. To Murray Dubin, for being my friend and confidant.

A special thanks to Brad Thomas, Judy Maher, P. J. Juhrend R.P.T., Cathy Smith M.A., Mark Fatum R.P.T., Mary Jane Smith, Sherri Hyatt, Joe Mika, and Racquetball World in Canoga Park, California, for assisting in creating this book. To all the people who were instrumental in the development of Wallyball. Although time and space do not permit me to mention everyone, I'd like to thank each and every one of you for your support.

Last but not least, to all the people across the country who play Wallyball—none of this would have been possible without you.

CONTENTS

PREFACE

I do not think anyone would argue with me if I claimed to be the only Puerto Rican ex-actor to have invented a new sport that boasts, after just five years, nearly a million players.

And now, with Wallyball growing faster every day, with leagues forming around the country, there has been a clamor for a book of rules, a book that tells how to play the game and how the game came to be played.

So here is the first official Wallyball book. It will explain that my game is basically the game of volleyball played on a racquetball court with the walls an essential part of the playing area. Four, six, or eight persons can play.

This book will explain that this is a game for the person who would rather walk out to shop than work out to stay in shape, a game for the Sunday softball player and the man or woman who was never big or strong enough to play competitive sports. It will also explain that the game can be difficult and competitive enough to lure the professional athlete into becoming a Wallyball fanatic.

But most importantly, this game is fun. I've seen Olympic volleyball players, men and women in wheelchairs, kids, old people, folks from Rapid City, South Dakota, to King of Prussia, Pennsylvania, play this game and have the time of their lives.

In fact, if you'll allow me to twist a famous Will Rogers line around, I've never met anyone who's played the game and not liked it.

So, don't take too long to read this book. Find some friends and get a game going. Wallyball is easy to learn and easier to play.

And I make you this promise: Wallyball is the most fun you can have with your shorts on.

Mr. Wallyball wouldn't lie.

INTRODUCTION

About the most famous thing in Calabasas, California, is the pet cemetery. The animals buried include Hopalong Cassidy's horse, Rudolph Valentino's pet Doberman, the ring-eyed dog from the Our Gang movies, and the pets of Henry Fonda, Alfred Hitchcock, and Humphrey Bogart.

So Calabasas has more than its share of dead dogs and cats and ponies and gerbils in the ground. It also has a man-made lake and some fancy houses, but not much else. Northwest of Los Angeles and not far from Malibu, Calabasas is hot in the summer and expensive year-round.

But it will always be a special place for me. Calabasas was the womb. It's where Wallyball began.

It was 1979, and I was the racquetball pro and the assistant manager of a racquetball facility that was under construction. I had become a good racquetball player in the years before, while I was trying to find work as an actor. Though I had landed minor parts in *The China Syndrome* and the television shows "Three's Company" and "Police Woman," I was out of work enough to spend five hours a day on the racquetball court. I decided that I could make more money delivering backhands than dialogue.

But interest in racquetball was already ebbing in 1979, and courts were empty around the country. So, on a hot summer afternoon, while the racquetball club was under construction, with beers in

In the spring of 1982, I had the pleasure of meeting Bud Mulhieson, the father of racquetball.

hand, the workmen and I were sitting around figuring out new games that could be played on a racquetball court.

The games we invented that afternoon (games that will be buried forever in Calabasas, with Valentino's Doberman) included the wonder of wiffle-ball-wall, the futuristic four-wall basketball, the sometimes risqué roller hockey ball (don't ask), and wall-wall tennis, which needs no explanation.

Like I said, there is not much to do in Calabasas on a hot summer afternoon.

But at home that night, another game came to mind: volleyball played on a racquetball court. Off-the-wall volleyball.

I tried it the next day with a racquetball and then with a leather volleyball. The workmen and I tied a string across the middle of the court about 8 feet high and it worked. We actually played, hitting the ball off the wall and over the net. Naming the sport proved more difficult than inventing it.

Ricochet Ball? Zoom Ball? Bullet Ball? None was right. I needed a perfect fit, and they all hung like loose suspenders. Several weeks later, at a backyard volleyball game, I suddenly realized what I had done. I had come up with a new game, a volleyball game with walls. There could only be one name that fit.

Wallyball was born.

But the baby had some problems. If you really hit the ball hard, it could easily bounce off two or three walls and be more like pinball than volleyball. That was no fun for the person trying to hit it. So I limited the number of walls the ball could strike.

Regulation volleyball is played with six players, and recreational volleyball is often played with more. That was too many people. Too often I had seen point after point played in volleyball with some players never touching the ball.

Wallyball had to be different. It had to involve every player on just about every point. No lulls, no dead time. Three or four on a team and no more. Play with two, if you really want a workout, but never more than four.

And the walls. They had to make the better player better, give the heavy hitter more ways to score a point. But they also had to be the great equalizer, deadening the rocket return and bouncing the weak hit up and over.

There were also other refinements, wrinkles that had to be smoothed. In the fall of 1979, two friends and I put together our combined wealth of $5,000 and started Wallyball, Inc. We did a patent search to make sure no one had already invented Wallyball and found, to our surprise, that people had played off-the-wall volleyball games in airplane hangars in the early 1900s. But no one had ever done anything with the game.

So we registered the Wallyball name, and I set up an office in my bedroom. Cardboard cartons were my filing cabinets. My phone answering machine was changed. Now it said: "Mr. Wallyball."

We had a name, a game, and the cocksure certainty of men with a better mousetrap. In early 1980, we took our newly made Wally-ball displays and brochures to a trade show in Anaheim, California. A fellow from a large sports equipment manufacturer suggested that a rubberized version of a volleyball might be the perfect ball for our game.

I shooed the engineer away. I had been an entrepreneur for at least four months, and I knew that volleyball players wouldn't play with anything but a leather ball. Fortunately, the man persisted and

Here I am
at a trade show
in Anaheim, California.

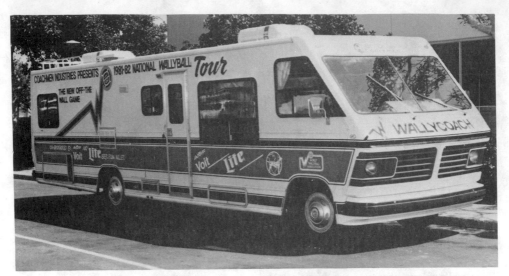

Coachmen Industries sponsored the Wallyball national tour of 1981–82
by providing us with the "Wallycoach."

made a rubberized, seamless ball. It gripped the walls and would dipsy-doodle right or left, depending on the spin.

It was perfect. We now produce thousands of Wallyball balls every year. Without his foresight, I might still be in Calabasas.

The game began to take off. Racquetball court managers liked it because it filled their empty courts. And, after the game, there were six or eight players drinking beer instead of two. I moved out of the bedroom and into the living room.

Nineteen eighty was our first year, and we sold about 200 Wallyball kits—ball, net, hardware—to racquetball facilities in the United States. We estimated that 15,000 people were playing. Today, we've sold kits to more than 2,800 racquetball centers and have estimated that nearly a million people are playing the game around the world.

Late in 1980, I needed more space and moved the office into the garage. In 1981, I moved into a real office. More than 90 percent of our sales were in the Midwest and East, and here I was in California, where I was finding it increasingly difficult to get the volleyball players off the beach and onto a racquetball court.

So, with the help of my brother, Jimmy, I planned a tour. Coachmen Industries sponsored the trip east and threw in a mobile home that we quickly named the "Wallycoach."

For five months in late 1981 and early 1982, my cat, Wally, and I drove 24,000 miles and visited 46 cities. On the road, my 32-foot motor home drew stares as drivers read the advertising signs on the side. I could see their mouths move: "What in the world is Wallyball?"

Amarillo, Texas. Omaha, Nebraska. Pittsburgh, Pennsylvania. Marietta, Georgia. Elkhart, Indiana. Denver, Colorado. Fort Lauderdale, Florida. Madison Heights, Michigan. Fremont, California. Rolling Meadows, Illinois. Helena, Montana. Seattle, Washington. St. Louis, Missouri. You name it, and I was there. I was the pied piper preaching this funny game, but people liked it. Crowds came to the racquetball courts. Local newspapers and television publicized my appearances. People invited me for dinner. Kids asked for my autograph. Everyone loved my game.

I came back to California in early 1982 and soon began to feel a financial crunch. We were selling lots of kits, but we had lots of expenses. And when the tour ended, some of the interest died down, too. The next couple of years are a blur of bad business decisions and doubts about the game ever really making it. At one point, I even walked away from it, tossed the game aside, and decided to get into another line of work.

But you know what? Wallyball is a weed, and it grew without me. Reporters kept calling me. Racquetball club managers kept phoning.

In 1984, I decided to give it one more shot. Mr. Wallyball was coming back.

Standing beside me is the Wallyball national spokesperson, Paul Sunderland, Olympic volleyball gold medalist, 1984.

Left to right:
Mr. Wallyball, Wilt Chamberlain, and Kevin Doyle (an early business partner).

Now I've got pros on the management end and sports figures like Olympic volleyballers Paul Sunderland and Rita Crockett on our team. Major corporations are underwriting the cost of leagues nationwide. Two hundred players began competing in a Los Angeles–area league in October 1985. A national league program will begin by the spring of 1986.

People wiser than I tell me they can see the day when Wallyball will be played inside portable glass courts with television cameras broadcasting the action around the world—maybe from Madison Square Garden.

Wallyball and I have come a long way from Calabasas. I've been asked by more than a few people why I stuck with it, why I believed in my strange game with the blue ball.

Ever see something and say to yourself, Hey, I should have thought of that? A lot of people have said that to me about Wallyball. It's so easy, so natural. Volleyball is so American, so full of pleasant images—picnics and beaches and good times. I'm so sure that Wallyball was meant to happen.

Now, there have been times when I've wanted to shake people and scream: "Play my game! It's fun. You'll like it. I promise you'll like it."

But those times have gone. I don't need to shake anyone anymore. Distinguished-looking men in jackets and ties compliment me on my business acumen and say, yes, their companies are interested in investing in Wallyball. When I get on the court to play, people point to me and murmur, "Isn't he the guy?"

Every shot I hit now—on the court, in life—seems to be a winner. It may not last, but you can't score if you don't stay in the game. I'm in it for the duration.

Who knows? Maybe one day, Calabasas will be famous for its dead Dobermans and for the game invented there one lazy, hot summer afternoon.

I
EQUIPMENT

There is one drawback to Wallyball: you can't play at home, or in the pool, or in your mother-in-law's backyard. Sorry, but you're going to have to play on a racquetball court.

With the help of Al Scates, the UCLA volleyball coach, Wallyball rules have been formulated. And the first one concerns where the game is played.

Play Wallyball on a standard handball or racquetball court. The two back walls should each be 20 feet high and 20 feet long. The two long walls should each be 20 feet high and 40 feet in length. The service area is a 3-foot-wide strip along each back wall.

The net height is 8 feet for men's play, 8 feet for coed play, and 7 feet, 4¼ inches for women's play.

Installing the net is very simple. The health and racquet club that you are playing at will probably have some, if not all, courts equipped with plates sunk into the wall at the appropriate height of 8 feet.

The ball is an official blue Wallyball. It should weigh between 9 and 10 ounces and have a circumference of 25 to 27 inches.

As for your clothing, don't wear anything that constricts your movement. Shorts and a shirt, sweats, your old basketball uniform from high school, or whatever else you feel comfortable perspiring in is OK.

Wear sneakers, of course, and it might not be a bad idea to put on some knee and elbow pads. You certainly don't *need* knee and elbow pads to play, but I've seen a lot of rookie players become so involved in the game that they're diving for balls and bumping into the walls their first time out.

If looking spiffy on the court is important to you, and trendiness is next to godliness in your home, an entire line of Wallyball clothes, duffel bags, knee and elbow pads, and visors is available. Everyone in Calabasas wears them.

2
THE GAME

OK, we're ready to Wally. But before we start, a little warming up is in order. Wallyball is a game of quick starts and stops, and I don't want anyone to pull anything. My minor league baseball coach in Miami (I was a catcher in a Dodgers' Class D team, and my career was, with good reason, brief) used to tell me: "Loose muscles are happy muscles."

Wallyball is a vigorous game and it's important to take about 10 minutes beforehand to stretch and loosen up. Take the time. You'll play better, you'll feel better, and your chance of injury will be lessened. (I also do about 10 minutes of practice after stretching; see the drills in Chapter 9.)

There are almost as many stretching exercises as there are people who need stretching.

The stretches on pages 16, 17, and 18 should be done slowly and easily, and each stretching motion should be held for a slow count of 10. Breathe normally.

Now we're all loose and ready to go. Wallyball can be played with four, six, or eight, but for this game there will be eight of us—four men and four women, divided into teams of two men and two women each. Each team has a man and woman in the front, near the net, and a man and woman in the back.

Like volleyball, Wallyball begins with the serve. The server may

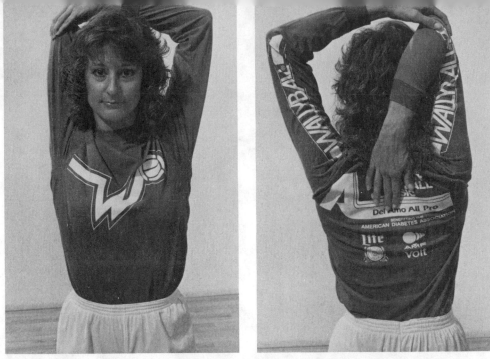

This is for your upper arms and shoulders. Stand straight, knees bent slightly. Bend your right arm behind your head, the elbow pointing up. Extend the right hand down to the shoulder blades. Put your left hand on the right elbow and tug down gently. You should feel the stretch in your upper arm and back. Repeat with the left hand.

For your chest and upper body, stand in the corner of the court, placing your hands on each wall, and slowly lean forward until you feel a stretch in your chest and arms.

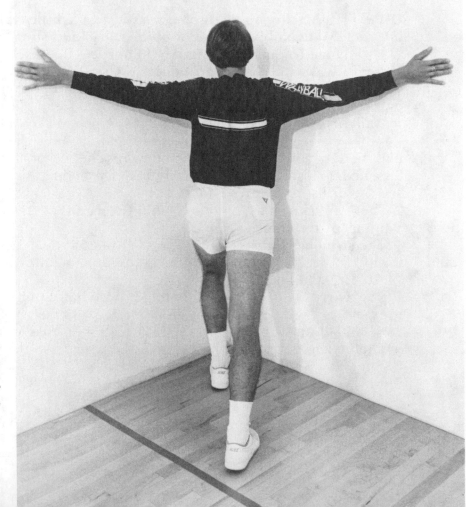

This is for your trunk. Your legs should be apart, knees bent. Put your right hand on your right outer thigh and your left hand straight over your head. Bend to the right slowly, sliding your hand to your knee. You should feel the left side of your body stretching. Repeat on the other side.

This is a stretch for your quadriceps and one you've probably done before. Stand with one knee bent behind you. Grasp your ankle and pull it toward your buttocks to the side. If balance is a problem, you may want to stand near a wall. Repeat with the other leg.

Extend a straight leg far enough to the side so that you feel a stretch in the inner thigh. Your other leg is bent. Rock toward that bent leg, stretching the thigh with every move. Repeat with the other leg extended.

This is great for your thighs and your back. For this one, you need two exercisers. Sit on the floor facing each other and extend your legs forward so that the soles of your feet touch the soles of your partner's feet. Join hands at the wrist. Now, taking turns, gently pull your partner toward you as you lean backward. Lean at the hips and try to keep your back straight. Do not stretch any farther than is comfortable.

Ready to play.

stand anywhere behind the three-foot line—right corner, left corner, center, anywhere. Feet off the line, please.

The serve is the most important shot in the game and can be hit directly over the net, off a wall and over the net, or over the net and off a wall. You can whack the ball as hard as you like, but the ball may not strike more than one wall and may not strike the other team's back wall at all. (More detailed instruction on serving will be provided in Chapter 5.)

If the ball hits the floor before it is returned, the serving team wins a point.

The receiving team can strike the ball as many as three times before it must be returned. Again, the ball can be shot over the net, off a wall and over the net, or over the net and off a wall. The same back wall prohibition applies.

One important item to be noted here is that the receiving team may strike the ball into the back wall under one condition—if it is the team's own back wall. I'll discuss later how a team can use its own walls.

Wallyball is like volleyball in many ways, but the scoring system is not one of them. Our system is better.

I've felt for a while now that volleyball games are too slow and have too many pointless rallies. In everything from tennis to Ping-Pong, a great shot is rewarded with a point, no matter who is

The server must always stand behind the service line when serving. You may lean over the imaginary plane of the service line, but your foot may not be touching or over the line before the ball is struck.

serving. In volleyball, only the great shot made by the serving team is rewarded with a point.

Wallyball is 21 points long, and the game is not over until the winning team has a 2-point advantage. A point is scored in every rally, no matter who is serving. Win the point and the serve is yours.

But when a team reaches 18 points, we slow down a bit and switch to volleyball rules for that team—and that team only. The team with 18 points now can score only when they're serving.

The other team is still scoring the old way, whether they are serving or not. It's a great way to give a team a chance to catch up.

When the losing team reaches 18 points, then it's volleyball rules for them, too.

The Federal International de Volleyball, the world governing body for volleyball, is currently testing this scoring system to determine whether volleyball will go the way of Wallyball.

After a change of serve, players rotate positions clockwise. Whether it be teams of two, three, or four, players must always rotate, and the next player in rotation serves.

In league play, a match is 3 games, and the first one to win 2 is the winner. But if you are playing with friends in a nonleague game and want to stay on the court longer, enjoy yourself. Play 8 games. Play 88 games. Hey, I'm Mr. Wallyball. Play as long as you want.

Simple, right? Well, it *is* simple. But as you get better at it, you'll learn that Wallyball has strategy and plays, special shots (you'll love the cobra) and devilish serves and a lot of moves, offensively and defensively, that don't seem possible within four walls.

Before we get to the tricky stuff, let's take a look at the fundamentals.

3
BASIC SKILLS

The three hits for the team receiving the serve are usually the return of serve or pass, the set, and the spike. That's the way Olympic volleyball and champion Wallyball players do it. I suggest you do it that way, too, but don't be afraid to experiment. Hit the ball over the net on the first shot if you can or spike it on the second shot or don't spike it at all—whatever works for you.

RETURNING THE SERVE

If you *can't* return the serve, however, you're in big trouble. And if you return it weakly, the setter will not be able to set it, and the spiker might as well stay home and play Trivial Pursuit.

Volleyball skills picked up in high school or at the playground will generally help you learn how to return a serve. Get ready by bending the knees slightly, keeping the legs about shoulder width apart, and watching the ball intently. Be ready to spring up if the ball comes at you high and hard off the wall or to get down low in a crouch if the server caroms one off the lower part of the wall.

Most serves are struck off a wall, which makes this game very different from volleyball. Quickly, you must follow the path of the ball and determine where on the wall it will strike and how far it will

The wrong way.
As you can see, she is not looking at the ball,
her legs are straight, and her feet aren't square.

The right way.
Notice the position of his feet,
his eye contact with the ball, and his bent knees.

bounce off. At that moment, high school geometry may be more useful than high school volleyball.

Before the serve, your feet were pointing toward the net—past tense. As soon as you realize that the ball is going to rebound off the wall, shift your feet away from the net and toward the wall. I cannot stress how important that shift of position is. I've seen Olympic volleyballers, marvelous athletes, try unsuccessfully to dig a shot off the wall while their feet—and, necessarily, their bodies—were still facing the net.

Now that you're in position, you have to hit the ball. The best way to return the serve and hit it to a teammate is with a forearm or bump pass. This pass works because you are creating a long, wide, flat surface with your forearms to hit the ball.

Let's make this clear. It's not your hands that hit the ball; it's your forearms. Forget about your hands. Now extend those valuable forearms in front of you, elbows down and hands together, the fingers of one in the palm of the other.

As for your hands, decide what is comfortable and what works

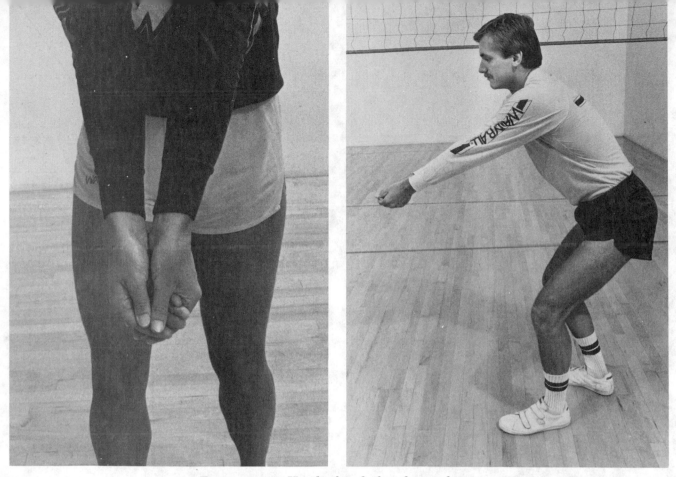

**Forearm pass. Hands closed, thumbs touching.
Remember, strike the ball with the forearms and not your hands.**

best for you. Placing the fingers of one hand in the palm of the other seems to be the best way, but there are variations on that position. Decide what is comfortable and what works best for you. You may put the fingers of one hand in the palm of the other and keep both hands open with the thumbs far apart. Or you may close the hands and have the thumbs touching and parallel. Another option is to have the hands partially closed with the thumbs parallel but not touching.

You have now created a flat surface, but it's resilient like a trampoline, not rigid like a board. The ball should strike both forearms at the same time and then be guided by your arms in the direction you want. If the elbows are bent, the ball will hit the forearms and fly back over your head. If your arms are pointed toward the floor, the ball will hit them and drop. If your elbows are straight and your arms are almost parallel to the floor, the ball should go where you want.

One last tip: Don't be intimidated by a screaming rocket serve off the wall. One, your forearms can take it; they'll "give" with the ball.

Setting. Eye contact is essential. Watch the ball into your hands, and make sure to use your fingertips and not your palms when hitting the ball. Keep your knees bent and step into ball in the direction you're planning to hit it.

Two, the walls are the great equalizer in Wallyball, softening even the most ferocious of shots.

SETTING

As important as the return of serve or forearm pass is, it is rare that the returner is good enough to hit the ball as accurately as needed to set up a spike. A middle step is needed, and that is the set or overhand pass.

Simply put, the set is a high, two-handed pass near the net to a teammate who jumps and slams the ball in midair over the net, often using a wall. It looks easy and almost effortless, but, of course, it's not. Like the player who gets the assists in basketball, the setter is noticed only when he or she makes a bad pass.

If there is a trick to setting the ball, other than lots of practice, it is that you must get directly under the ball. Not right or left, but smack-dab in the middle, ready for the ball to hit you in the face or chest if you should miss it.

But you're not going to miss it. You have moved quickly to where the ball was hit by your teammate. Your head is up, and your hands are spread and above your head. Shoulders are squared and pointed in the direction you want the ball to go. Elbows are out, knees are bent, and one foot is slightly ahead of the other, pointing in the direction you want to hit it.

The hands start out spread but get closer together, with the tips of the thumbs almost touching as the ball comes closer—and closer. The fingers are cupped. Contact. The ball hits the fingertips and thumbs—not the palms—simultaneously.

The ball is struck with the fingers and thumbs, but the whole body gets into the act. Everything from ankles to elbows is involved as you hit the ball with almost a springing action of the hands and arms, then straighten up and follow through with the body.

SPIKING

OK, the setter has set it, and the ball is hanging in the air. There's only one hit left. You're the closest player to the ball, so it's your play, pal. The pressure's on.

The spiker probably has the toughest job on the Wallyball court. As the spiker, you have to be able to run and jump, time a leap with a moving ball, slam a ball hard or dink it softly, controlling where both of those shots land, and be ready to play defense—perhaps even blocking a spike—the moment after the ball is hit.

Spiking sequence. Keep your eye on the ball and make sure not to hit the net with any part of your body. That would be considered a fault, and you would lose the point.

Besides all that, the actual striking of the ball is far more difficult than it looks. Consider:

- If you strike the ball while it is still rising, there's a good chance that you will hit it too hard and against the back wall.
- If you strike the ball too late on its fall downward, you are likely to hit it into the net or, heaven forbid, swing and miss.
- If you jump too late or too soon, you become out of synch with the ball and lose your momentum.

Ideally, the ball is struck at the magic moment when it is hanging there, having ended its ascent and just beginning its descent.

As the setter is about to set, you should be anticipating and moving forward. As the ball leaves the setter's hands and lofts upward, you have stopped your run and begun your jump. You are behind, not under, the ball as you leap and swing your arm forward like a hammer. Contact with the ball is made with the heel of the hand (not the fist). The rest of the hand and fingers follow forward.

In most cases, the best place for the spiked ball to land is low on a side wall, a most difficult shot to return.

Timing the leap, striking the ball cleanly, controlling where the ball goes, and recovering quickly into a defensive position make the spiker the acrobat, slugger, quarterback, and shot blocker in Wallyball.

4

POSITIONING

We've now gone over how the game was developed, the equipment needed, the fundamentals of play, and the three shots most often used.

So, if you go out on the court now, you will be ready to play—except for one thing. No one's told you where to stand after you go out on the court. We still have to discuss positions. Like the doubles team in tennis, Wallyballers have specific places to stand, special areas of responsibility. And because of the constant rotation of positions during a game, you have to know not only the position you start out at, but every other position as well.

In our league play, we recommend that newcomers to Wallyball with little or no volleyball experience play four on a side. Those who have played Wallyball for a year or more or who have played organized volleyball are generally put into either threes or fours, depending on their preference. The very best players, those with three years of Wallyball experience or college volleyball veterans, play twos or threes.

This is a new game, and strategies are still evolving, but, for now, what follows are the accepted positions for teams of two, three, and four players. Again, if you can figure out a better way and it works for you and your team, go for it.

Twos. The player with the stronger net skills may want to position himself or herself closer to the net for a possible spike.

TWOS

Two players versus two players is the most tiring form of Wallyball. The court may not seem that big, but it seems to stretch out when you're playing doubles, or twos.

There are several position variations in twos. I know players who have experimented with one up and one back, both in the center of the court. And I've seen one up and one back, with the teammates leaning toward opposite side walls. But the way that seems to work best is two back, on opposite sides, about three-quarters deep in the court.

It is easier to run forward than to run back, so playing a little deep makes sense. It's also easier to return a shot off the wall when the ball is in front of you. In two deep, each player is responsible for the side he or she is closest to, except for one important and infrequent shot.

Returning a fast shot off a wall is, in many cases, easier for the player standing farthest from the wall that the ball struck. In our illustration of position, the man would play balls caroming off the wall nearest the woman, and the woman would play balls crashing into the wall near her teammate.

Incorrect position.
Half of the court is left uncovered.

Correct position.
Both halves of the court are covered.

There *are* situations where you play the carom on your side, but they will be covered when we talk more about playing twos in later chapters.

One last point: If you do choose to play with one up and one back, you must be sure that the player closer to the net does not block the opponent's view of the server, which could subject your team to a penalty. (See Chapter 11, "Wallyball Rules," for details.) Whether the game is twos, threes, or fours, the opposing team always must have a clear view of the server.

One up, two back. The strongest spiker should be closest to the net.

THREES

Playing threes, or triples, is my favorite way to play. I'm getting too old to run around as much as you ought to in twos. I can't say anything bad about fours because it's a great game, too: if chocolate ice cream is your favorite, then fours is lots of chocolate ice cream. However, threes is lots of chocolate chocolate chip.

When you play threes, you get the best of both worlds. In fours, play consists mostly of bumping, setting, and spiking. In twos most of the time a player is trying to cover all the empty space on the court and often spends much of his time on the floor diving to save the ball. Threes is a happy medium. There is the running and diving of twos and the more finesse stuff of setting and spiking as in fours—it makes for a great workout.

I've seen just two strategies for positioning a team for a game of triples. There are not a great many ways to move three people around that make sense.

In the first, one player is at the net, with two back. In the second, two players are at the net, with one back. It has been my experience, as the longest active Wallyball player in the free world, that the set-up of two up and one back doesn't work. Playing just one back runs that rear player ragged. It's also too easy to serve a winner with just one person back.

There are, however, times during a game when a switch from one up and two back to two up and one back may work to your advantage. For instance, the other team's server has been devastating, and your team would like to put on some added pressure. So you move an extra player up front as a potential serve blocker. It might work once or twice and may shift the momentum. And it may make the server worry more about where his or her opponents are standing instead of where the serve is going.

But don't overdo your receiving rotation during service reception. Keeping just one player back, even if that person is a combination Rambo and Baryshnikov, is asking for trouble.

In terms of exact position, the two back Wallyballers should stand just in front of the service line, each a couple of feet away from a side wall. But those positions are not static. For instance, if the server is hitting everything off the left wall, then the defensive player closer to the right wall should consider cheating toward the middle to play the carom. And the defensive player next to the left wall might get even closer to it—make believe you're wallpaper—in an effort to return the ball before it hits the wall.

The net player in threes usually stands at the middle of the net, about an arm's length away. But, as you'll note in our illustration, the net player has cheated to the side of the net where the server has been hitting the ball.

FOURS

Fours is the most social of Wallyball games. It is the two-couple, neighbor versus neighbor, buddy versus buddy, mother versus daughter game, the game where there seem to be as many giggles as good hits.

Now don't get me wrong. I've seen and competed in some killingly competitive fours games. Some of the best Wallyballers prefer fours, enjoying the many variables and the different moves that can be made offensively and defensively.

The diamond.

Two-two. Communication among players is very important with this positioning.
Don't let the middle of the court go uncovered.

One up, three back. Again, you want your strongest spiker up front.

One of those variables is how to line up. There are three viable ways to position your team in fours. First, there is the two-two, two players up at the net and two back. Second is the diamond, with one player up, two on the sides, and one deep. The third is one up and three back, almost the same as the diamond.

Each of these positions has its own proponents. Brad Thomas, a friend in Detroit who is one of the best Wallyballers in Michigan and arguably one of the top players in the nation, says that two-two is the best way to play. Other friends say Brad has inhaled too many gasoline fumes and argue for the diamond or one-three.

One argument against the diamond is that the back player often does not see the ball very much. And one argument for two up and two back is that your team always has two blockers at the net ready to get in the way of the server or to block a spike.

Now, I can also argue for the diamond and one-three because they both can work well against the dominant server. But, for the moment, excuse me if I punt the whole subject. Hey, I love Wallyball, but going into the intricacies of the two-two versus the one-three is a little much. This is a game with four walls, a net, and a ball. It's easy to play. Let's not intellectualize it too much. Stand anywhere you want to on the court. We'll talk a little more about strategy later (see Chapter 7).

5
SERVING

The spiker may have the most difficult job on the Wallyball court, but the server's is the most important. With a good server in the game, the returner won't return, the setter won't set, and the spiker will never get the chance to spike.

In the same way that good pitching usually prevails over good hitting in baseball, an outstanding server will dominate in Wallyball. I've seen servers beat good teams 15–0. I've seen servers who were unhittable, whose serves dipped like knuckleballs and spun like cue balls. I've seen servers who constantly outthought the opposition, serving where they weren't. And I've seen servers with such great ball control that they could smash paper cups on the opponent's court—using the side walls, of course.

The serve is another major difference between the games of volleyball and Wallyball. Serving in volleyball is certainly important, but rarely will you see a 15–0 volleyball game due to a super server. Remember, volleyball usually has six players, and that makes it more difficult for the server to find an open area to dominate the game. In both games, a good server should be able to put the ball anywhere on the opponent's side of the court. But in Wallyball, "anywhere" includes the side walls. And if the walls in Wallyball tend to keep the tall, heavy hitter from dominating, they add another weapon for the talented server.

Foot fault.

Good serve.
Notice your foot can be in the air
(over the line) as you strike the ball.

OK, as we've said before, the server may stand anywhere behind the serving line. Your foot cannot touch the line anytime during the serve. It can, however, be in midair above and over the line, as long as you serve the ball before your foot touches the floor.

UNDERHAND SERVES

The underhand serve is commonly used by beginners. It's a good way to control the ball, get it over the net, and put it where you want on the court.

Face the net with knees bent and your left foot forward if you're a right-hander, right foot forward if you're a lefty. I'm a right-

Underhand serve. Strike the ball with the palm of the hand.

hander, as shown in the photos, and the following instruction is for right-handers (just switch hands if you're a lefty).

Hold the ball in front of you, about waist high, with your left hand. Swing your right hand back behind you like a pendulum and then swing it forward, striking the ball with the heel of your hand. You can hit the ball open-handed, or with your fingers closed in a fist. Use whichever way feels more comfortable and then practice it. Continue looking at the ball in your hand as contact is made. Step forward with your right foot as your arm swings through.

The perfect serve, underhand or overhand, just skims across the top of the net. Lobs are a good shot in tennis, but not in Wallyball. Try keeping your head down, looking at the ball. It may help you keep that underhand serve low.

OVERHAND SERVE

Overhand is the way most Wallyballers serve. Again, stand facing

Overhand serve. Similar to throwing a ball,
it's important to step in the direction you want
the ball to go and to have a smooth follow-through.

Overhand serve. When you toss the ball it should be on the imaginary plane above your front foot, which would be right above the service line.

the net with your left foot (if you are a righty) ahead a bit. Ideally, it would be nice to toss the ball with both hands to control it better, but no one seems to use both hands. With your weight distributed evenly on both feet, toss the ball with your left hand. The toss should be about three feet in the air and in front of your right shoulder.

Your hitting hand should be back behind your head, cocked and ready to come forward. Your elbow leads the way, and the arm, fairly straight at the moment of contact, follows through. Strike the ball in its center with the heel of your hand. Your feet, of course, must stay off the service line. A winner!

The importance of the toss cannot be stressed too strongly. As in tennis, if the ball is tossed too high and struck at a point higher in the air than you would like, the serve will go too high or too long. The same result may await you if you strike the upper part of the ball. Tossing the ball too low or striking the ball on its lower half will generally mean the ball will go into the net.

Now the tricky stuff starts.

SPIN SERVES

The blue ball in your hands is a living thing, a Frankenstein creation that will do your bidding. It will jump when you tell it, go right, go left, dip—behave in any way you command.

Remember, Wallyball is not a game for behemoths, but rather for those of agile feet and mind. It is more finesse than power. So, when the other team expects you to serve a ball that zigs, make sure it zags. When your opponents expect you to bang one off the wall, freeze them with a "wallpaper job."

The ball will spin not only off the walls, but also off an opponent's forearms, making it that much harder to pass. If you really want to make the ball dance, you ought to know how to spin a serve.

Backspin and Topspin

The ball will die or drop like a rock if you use backspin. In much the same way that a cue ball reacts to being struck low, the Wallyball will die after it hits a wall when backspin is applied.

If you strike the lower part of the ball and send your serve into a side wall, the ball will jump downward after contact with the wall. No carom; just a dip down. And it is difficult to get low enough to return such a shot. With topspin, the opposite occurs. The ball is struck in the upper half, and, instead of dying as it hits a wall, it comes alive, spinning toward the back wall.

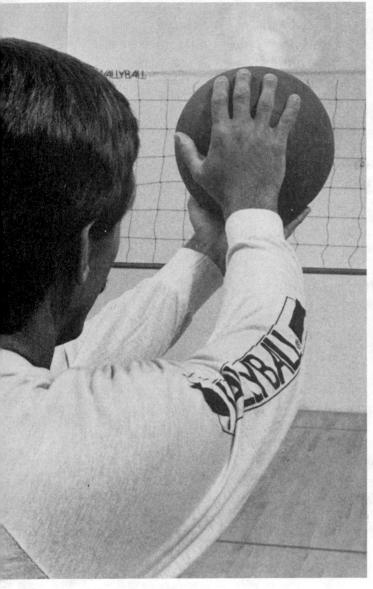

Ordinary serve.

Right-hand spin serve.

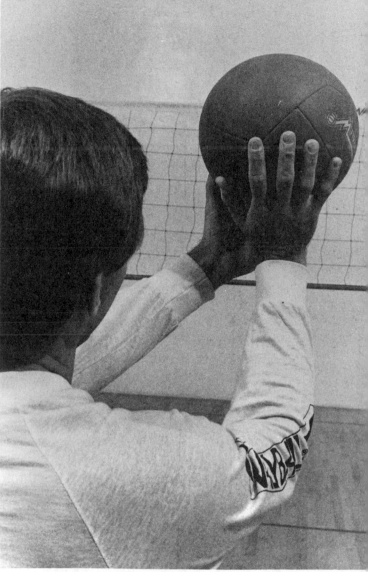

Left-hand spin serve.   Backspin serve.

Right and Left Spins

If you're standing on the right side of the court and serving toward the left wall, you might use left-to-right or clockwise spin to make the ball jump out from the wall and toward the net. If you were to use counterclockwise or right-to-left spin, the ball would jump out and then back toward the rear wall.

OK, we've talked about how to hit the ball. Now the question is where to hit it.

HITTING DIFFERENT SPOTS

The best place to hit the ball is crosscourt, an inch or two over the net, striking the side wall as close to the floor as you can (no higher than three or four feet) and as deep as you can, in the last one-third or one-fourth of the court.

Though that may be the best serve, the magic spot on the court that is most difficult to defend, it should not be your only serve. Even a good fastball pitcher throws a curve or change-up once in a while.

Remember, the object of serving is not to hit the ball, but to hit spots on the court. Quarterbacks often talk about attacking the seams of a defense, and a Wallyball server must do that, too.

If the other team is playing a one-two defense in triples, and the two players in the back are too deep, a shallow crosscourt serve may work perfectly.

If you've been banging serves against the right wall with lots of spin, you might want to change up and toss up a wallpaper serve, one that hugs the right wall—no carom, no spin—until it falls deep in the right corner.

The only limitations on serves are your imagination and the back wall. Deep off the side wall, shallow off the side wall. Topspin deep off the side wall, backspin deep off the side wall. Deep middle serve hitting no walls, little dink serve with backspin to the side. Deep middle serve with spin. . . . I can go on and on. And all of these serves change depending on where the server is standing.

The speed of the serve is less important than where it lands on the court and its spin. In fact, the harder a ball is struck on a spin serve, the less time the ball will have to spin. I'm not suggesting that you throw a marshmallow up there, but please understand that there's no reason to hit an out-of-control rocket, either.

Now, after your beautiful serve, you cannot stand around, watching your artistry. You have to be ready to play, to dig out a return, and even to hustle to the net and spike or block. (In fours only, the server is not allowed to spike or block.)

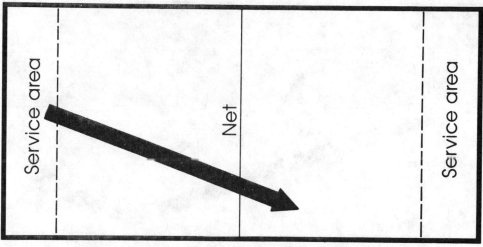

Short dink serve— ball is hit softly over the net, no spin.

Wallpaper serve.

Deep middle serve off the side wall.

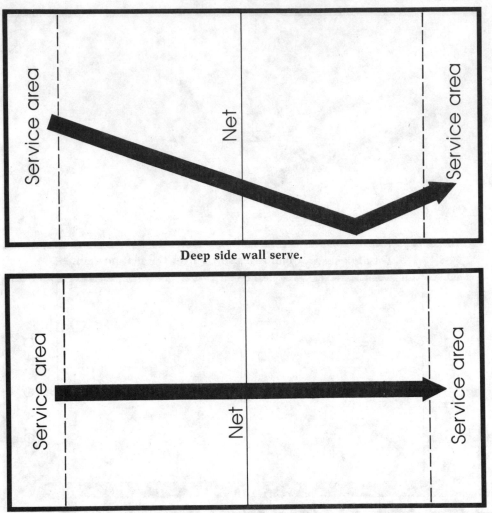

Deep side wall serve.

Deep middle back serve.

6
PLAYING THE BALL

It's time to make some shots, block some spikes, dig some serves, kick some. . . . Sorry, I got carried away. But I'm anxious to talk about the actual playing of the game and what you can and cannot do. So here's a nugget of net play, a dollop of dinks, and other shots I have known and loved.

HITS

What You Can't Do

Let me begin by telling you about some things that cannot be done when you hit the ball. First, you cannot hit it to yourself. You may be the best player on your team, but there are no one-man teams in Wallyball. If you hit it, someone else must hit it next. If you hit a great set, but the spiker falls and breaks an ankle, it may be a heartbreaker, but you cannot spike the ball yourself.

Nor can you touch a ball twice in succession. (There are two exceptions to this, which I'll discuss shortly.) So, if an opponent hits a serve that strikes you in the head, that is a legit hit, and your teammates can play the ball off your body. But you cannot.

Speaking of hitting, you cannot push, carry, hold, lift, scoop, or catch the ball with your teeth. You have to hit it.

**Illegal hit.
Hands open during an
underhand pass is considered
"carrying the ball" and is
a fault.**

Dinks

Sometimes the spiker, as a change of pace or because the other team is playing deep, will hit the ball softly—dink it—over the net rather than slam it against a side wall.

Dinking is fun and is the equivalent of the little seeing-eye squibbler that just makes it through the infield. It makes your opponent go, "Aarggh."

There are a lot of ways to dink, but the one way that you cannot do it is with an open hand. That's a fault, and the other team gets the ball. You may dink with your knuckles, with your fist, with the heel of your hand, or with the knuckles and back of your hand.

You may also dink with a cobra. Someone decided that, when you hold your arm and hand out parallel to the floor and curl your fingers, the shape of your hand looks like a cobra. (How would it sound if you told people about a garter snake shot?) Anyway, lots of players like to dink using a cobra. I take responsibility for the Wallyball name, but I had nothing to do with the cobra.

Dink with back of hand.

Dink with knuckles.

Illegal open-handed dink.

The cobra.

Dink with a fist.

The cobra lives at the net. You can
strike the ball softly for placement. Or
you can hit it with more authority,
which will produce a knuckleball effect—
making the ball jump all over.

The cobra is actually an easy shot to hit. With your hand cupped, and your knuckles facing the ceiling, bend your arms and strike the ball with the tips of your fingers. A good cobra shot can be a good dink shot and, if hit with a little more authority, can have the effect of a knuckleball in baseball—jumping all over the place.

When you develop a good cobra you don't have to hit it as a third shot. If you have position and you see an open spot, use it on the first or second shot.

NET PLAY

Net play is like line play in football. The trenches. Nose to nose, knuckle to knuckle, nylon netting the scrimmage line. "Spike it up his nose, Jim." "In your face."

I'm exaggerating. As I've said, Wallyball is not a game for the Wilt Chamberlains of the world, though I hear Wilt plays a mean game of Wallyball. You don't have to be big to play at the net or anywhere else on the court. Brad Thomas, the Detroit player I mentioned earlier, is 5'10" and plays a powerful and, more importantly, smart net game.

As for contact, if players from opposite teams leap for the ball their hands and arms may touch. It's competitive up there, but I've always felt that Wallyball somehow lacked the pressure of a game like tennis or basketball. Remember, this is fun.

OK, now some rules around the net.

First, don't touch it. Period. Not your uniform, not your little finger, not your nose hairs—nothing. If your momentum takes you into the net, too bad, Charley. The only way it is legal for your body and the net to get together is for the net to hit you. That may sound farfetched, but it happens when the ball strikes the net and moves it into a player.

By the way, if a ball hits the net, it is still alive and can be hit again, as long as it hasn't yet hit the floor.

As for above the net, well, the air is free, and you're entitled to your share of it. You can jump above the net and block a spike, serve, or any other shot. And you may also jump above and *over* the net, crossing that invisible plane, on two occasions: to block a spike or any other shot and when your own momentum carries you over after the ball has been struck on your own side, but remember, under no circumstance can you hit the net—not even touch it.

But you cannot, as illustrated in the photo, jump above and over the net to block the setting pass of the other team. You cannot block any pass. But if that set crosses the invisible line above the net, it becomes a free ball, and you can swat it.

Don't touch the net. It's considered
a fault and your team loses the point.

Don't run into the net.

Legally over the net, blocking a spike.

Illegal hit. It is considered
a foul to hit your opponent's set.

Legal block. Team spiking the ball loses point.

Retrieving a ball under the net. You may step on the line parallel with the net, but may not cross it.

Illegally crossing under the net.

If you're at the net trying to block a shot, your block is not considered one of your team's three hits. You may also hit the ball twice consecutively during a block.

You may also hit the ball more than once when you're playing a hard-spiked ball. That's the other exception to the rule. Let's say you're trying to dig an opponent's rocket spike deep in the corner. You're low, in good position, but the ball is spinning and bounces off your forearm and into your shoulder. In any other situation, that counts as two hits and a pass to yourself. The ball is dead.

But it's OK if you're playing a powerfully hit spiked ball. It's live, and you can hit it again. Obviously, your version of a hard-hit ball may be another person's dink. Arguments do arise. In league play, it's the referee's call. Otherwise, the players are going to have to make the call themselves.

Sometimes, the ball is hanging up there above the net like a balloon. Two opponenets at the net leap for it and end up catching it. They don't want to catch it. One is trying to spike it through to China, and the other is trying to block it, but four hands grab at the ball at the same moment and no one lets go. It's a held ball. The referee calls for a replay of the point. It does not happen a lot, but don't say I didn't prepare you.

THE CEILING

Speaking of above the net, well, what's really above the net? The answer is the ceiling.

Volleyballers on the beach, at a picnic, or in the Olympics do not have to contend with ceilings. They do have to worry about running after errant shots and loose balls, but ceilings do not concern them. Well, ceilings are part of the playing area in Wallyball.

If you're on the offensive team and you hit a ball into the ceiling and it lands back on your side, the ball is good and considered live. (If you somehow hit the ball into your own ceiling and then over the net, the shot is a fault.) If you hit the ball into the other team's ceiling, it's also a fault.

ERRANT SHOTS

As for under the net, errant shots may be retrieved, but you must be very careful not to interfere with an opposing player or to cross the line on the floor that runs from wall to wall parallel to the net. You can reach under the net to retrieve a shot. Remember your feet cannot cross the line, but they may touch it.

7
STRATEGY

People wise in the ways of sports books told me that I had to have a strategy chapter in my Wallyball book. If I didn't, said the wise guys, the readers would think any bozo can play the game. But the truth is that any bozo *can* play my game. That's the way I want it.

But I guess if you want to plan defenses, use a chalkboard, compute statistics and consider probabilities, you might as well do it playing Wallyball. If you're the kind of sports fan who's always screaming that the manager doesn't bunt enough or that the coach blitzes too often on third and long, hey you'll love Wallyball.

As for me, my skin breaks out when I start thinking too much. I can live without all this devious planning. But if you want it, here it is.

WATCH THE SERVER

Whether you're playing twos, threes, or fours, the way you return the serve will probably indicate how well you're going to do.

One tip I give players is to watch the server. The server is in full view and cannot hide. Remember, none of the offensive players can screen the server from your view. So watch where the server is standing and how he or she hits the ball. If you do, you should have a good idea of what's coming.

Playing close to the wall to get the best possible position on the ball as you can.

Playing too close to the wall.

Most servers hit crosscourt. You can see the server's hand and know if it's a right-hand spin, or left-hand spin, or no spin at all.

Receiving that tough off-the-wall serve is no picnic, but it's not impossible. First, you really have to get under the ball. Get your butt down. You have already pivoted so that your feet are facing the wall. It's at this moment when you have to make that split-second decision: get it off the wall or get it before it hits the wall.

Generally, you start out playing balls off the wall until the server proves to you that he or she is unhittable that way. Then you get close to the wall, planting your shoulder next to it like a plaster appendage. Now, a good server will notice your new relationship to the side wall and challenge you by hitting the ball more shallow on the wall so that it bounces in front of you. If the server puts a little

Climbing walls is illegal.

backspin on it, the ball will drop and die in front of you. It's not all easy bounces in Wallyball.

WALL CLIMBING

One thing you cannot do to get close to those walls is to climb them. Baseball outfielders can climb walls to get to the ball, but Wally-ballers cannot. You can rub against them, but you cannot propel yourself up a wall with your feet to get a ball.

POSITIONS

I talked about the different positions in fours earlier and compared the two-two and the diamond. One simple reason for playing the two-two is that it is often confusing having more than two people playing the ball off the wall. Sometimes, it's hard even having two.

**Sometimes two
is too many.**

Three people playing back can work, but they have to be a cohesive, experienced unit. It's terribly important for teammates to talk to one another and, if you're serious about Wallyball and want to participate in league play, to practice and play together.

One of the common misconceptions about Wallyball is that the player at the net—whatever the game or alignment is—is the blocker and spiker for his or her team.

Not necessarily. The player at the net generally is the blocker, but quite often the net player is also the setter, and one of the diggers is the spiker. So the digger returns the serve and passes it. The net player may receive the pass and set it to the digger, who is bounding forward to get ready for a spike over the net.

One of the things a good team tries to do against a good server is put two blockers at the net. George Cassius's New York teams are already known for often using two blockers when playing triples.

Now, that blocker at the net is trying to do two things. First, of course, he or she is trying to block the serve. Second, the blocker is trying to make that server think twice, to pull the trigger twice and maybe misfire. Obviously, there is a disadvantage in leaving just one man back to dig the serve, but there are times when the move is a good one.

SETTING

Setting is much more than just a high floating pass to a spiker. It is one of the delicious moments of strategy within every Wallyball point.

For instance, a setter can set high, letting the opposing team and the spiker see the developing play. But, a setter also can set very

Setting is one of those delicious moments of strategy in Wallyball. Change the height of your sets to keep the other team off balance.

low, just getting it barely above the net with the spiker hitting it quickly, before anyone on the opposition realizes that they have fallen victim to the Wallyball equivalent of the quick pitch.

A setter can set it right or left, depending on where the opponents' blockers are. A setter can back-set it to flying teammates. One fakes a spike; the other slams it.

The combinations are endless, and the defense changes as a team's choice of sets becomes apparent. In fours, for example, a team may switch to a one up-three back defense against a high-setting offense.

Be quick on your feet and always try to play aggressively at the net.

OFFENSE AND DEFENSE

More than once on a lazy Sunday afternoon in front of the television, I've made believe that I'm the quarterback. Second and long. The linebackers are blitzing, but I don't care. I knew they were coming and called a short flare pass to the halfback. Long gainer. Then a burst up the middle by the fullback. I notice the free safety is coming up fast to stop the run, so I call a flea flicker. It freezes the free safety while I throw a touchdown to the split end cutting across the middle.

Winning in competitive sports has always been a high for me. That win is invariably a combination of playing better and playing smarter than my opponent. Sports are often an athletic chess match, and figuring out what to do and when to do it can be as important as doing it.

Maybe that's why Wallyball seems the ideal game. You need ability, but you also have to be bright enough to know what tactics to use and when to use them.

We may not have blitzing linebackers or pinch hitters in Wallyball, but we've got moves. It doesn't matter whether you're playing a pickup game of doubles or a league match of three on a side. There are always moves to be made, strategy to be employed, variations to be tried. Hey, if you're dynamite and can dig, set, and spike equally well, you might get by on your talent alone. But, if you're like the rest of us, you might need an edge.

When I invented Wallyball, I didn't have a clue about how complicated a game it could be. I've said this is an easy game, and it is, but you can draw Xs and Os and little arrows in Wallyball just like they do at football games. However, I get a rash when people get too caught up in the Xs and Os of plays and strategy. I'm a simple fellow. I like to get out and play.

At first, I thought I would discuss offense and then defense. Wallyball isn't usually that neat. It's a fluid game where offense and defense are changing constantly. A server serves and he or she is on offense. The serve is blocked and suddenly the serving team is on defense. Throughout the course of a single point, offense and defense are constantly blurred.

Fours Offense

Fours is perhaps the most popular way to play Wallyball, although sometimes it's a little complicated coordinating and moving around that many people. Good fours teams practice a lot so that players don't trip over one another. Sometimes, one player may not see the ball that much in fours. You'd better submerge those egos if you want to have a successful fours team.

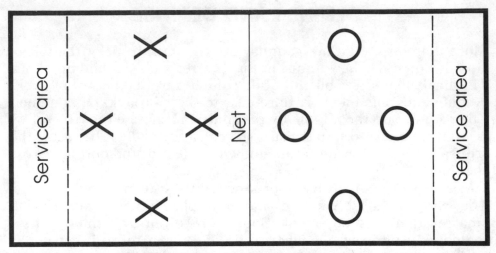

Four on four, using the diamond position.

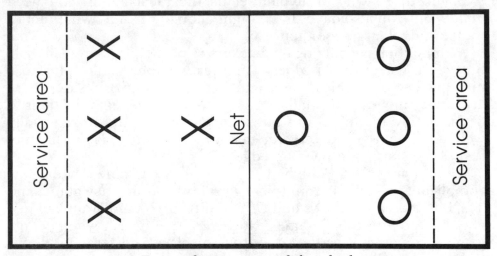

Four on four, one up and three back.

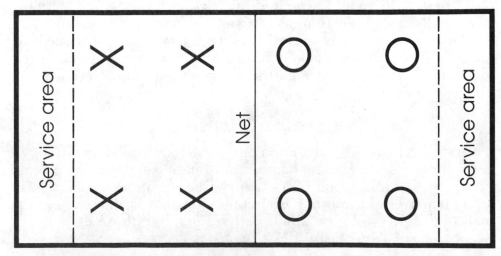

Four on four, two up and two back. Make sure to guard the middle of the court.

There are only two significant rules differences between fours and threes. In fours, the server may not spike or block a shot at the net. And in fours, the teams must maintain their clockwise rotation positions—don't move—until the server serves. In threes, if you want, you can line up in any position but you must maintain proper serving order. You can switch positions as the server is preparing to serve. In fours, you can't.

Two up and two back is the common fours formation. Placement of the ball is very important. In fours, you try to hit the places between, in front of, and behind the opposing players. You're aiming for the seams, the magic spots where the ball falls between opponents, leaving them only to protest.

"I thought you had it."

"Me! It was your ball!"

With four players, the setter has even more games to play. He or she can set to more people going in more directions at more speeds than in twos or threes. Also, you can have two setters so that you don't fall into patterns and have the same setter setting to the same spiker every play.

Fours Defense

With fours, you can always have at least one player in a spiker's face. With two players back, the only shot that will really hurt you is the crushing spike. If the offense has two spikers rushing the net, then you use two to meet and greet them.

If a spiker is beating you, double-team him. Make him or her hit it differently. Maybe the setter will set it to someone else. Another formation that a fours defense can use is three up front. It's not something you want to do too often because the one player in the back is in for big trouble if he or she has to play solo for 15 points. But it can work sometimes. You can use it once or twice, double-teaming one spiker and playing the other one on one, and then fake the same move later.

The fours defense can go a lot of ways: it can play an honest two-two, double-team a hot hitter, triple-team the net, or be sneaky and even slide a player back and play three deep.

Threes Offense

As I said earlier, having one player at the net and two back is probably the best formation. The net player has two jobs. First, this player is the blocker when his or her team is receiving the serve. The net player stands on the side of the court opposite the side that the server is on and tries to block the serve.

Remember, the serve is the ultimate weapon in Wallyball, and a good server will just chew you up. Someone has to be ready to block the serve or, at least, threaten to block it. Block that serve

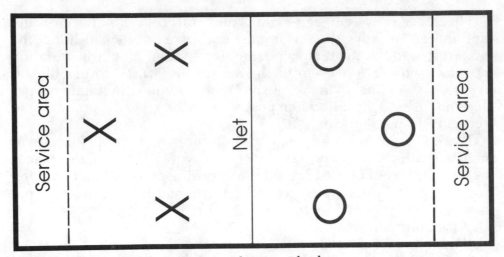

Three on three, one back.

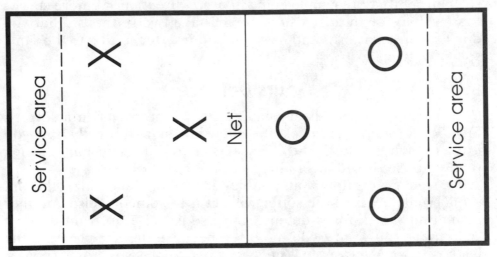

Three on three, one up.

once or twice, and you'll make the server think twice. Maybe the server will aim higher off the wall or change the direction of the serve completely.

For the unromantics among you, Wallyball is a game of angles, and the blocker's job is to alter the angle and stop that perfect low serve three-quarters down the side wall.

Blocking is no picnic. It requires great timing, jumping ability, and good instincts. But it is only one of the net player's jobs. The other task is to be the setter. That's right. Once the serve gets past the net player, one of the two back players will dig it and pass it toward the net. The receiver of that pass is the hustling blocker who has run toward the center of the net.

The setter is the quarterback of the team, the controller of the ball. That player decides how to set and to whom to set. He or she can set high or low, right or left, or fool everyone and shoot.

The two back players can both rush the net from opposite sides for a potential spike. Or one can rush the net. Or one can fake a rush and the other take the spike. There are lots of options.

I've said that just about every hit in Wallyball is the result of a pass, set, and spike. That's true, but it is not written in concrete. Nowhere in our rule book does it say you have to hit it three times. If your teammate makes a great dig and passes it nicely to the net for a set, it's OK if the setter spikes it instead of setting it. Very often, you'll see the other team watching the first two hits to see how the point is developing and where the third shot might go. They're watching the first two shots, not anticipating a shot right now. A shot on the second hit generally shakes the other team up and will keep them guessing the entire game.

Of course, there is nothing wrong with hitting it over on the first shot. The problem is that you'll rarely find yourself in a good enough position to hit a winner on the first hit. I can remember a few lollipop serves that I've been able to return on the first shot, but they haven't happened too often. Unless it's a real duck, I'd suggest at least one pass.

Threes Defense

In threes defense, one player should be at the net ready to block the serve. Since most players serve crosscourt, the net player is on the side of the court opposite to that of the server.

The two players back are midway between the net and the back wall. One is behind the net player and close to the wall, ready to dig the low serves and the wallpaper jobs. The other player is in the center, ready to return the high ricochets off the wall that rebound in the middle. The second player cannot forget that there are two side walls. If the server suddenly gets tricky and bounces one off the other wall, it's the middle player's play.

The one up–two back is a fine formation, but you may want to switch to a two up–one back if the other team is spiking you to death. Having a two-person block should discourage even the best spikers.

Twos Offense

If I were writing a book just about playing twos, I'd call it *Naked Wallyball*. There's nowhere to hide when playing twos. In threes or fours, teammates can cover for a player with limited skills. But in twos, a weak passer, setter, or spiker cannot avoid the ball. You really have to be adept at all phases of the game to play twos well.

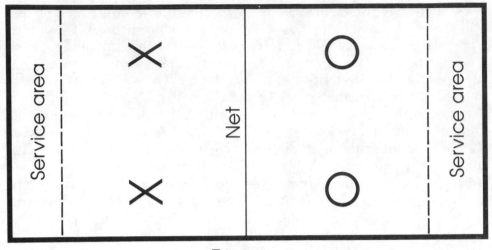

Two on two.

In fact, if you're new at Wallyball, I'd caution you not to try twos right away. Threes and fours are better games for getting accustomed to Wallyball and for practicing your skills. Only the best Wallyballers play twos well; for everyone else, it can be a frustrating experience. For those who do have some experience, here's some stuff on twos.

Two back is the way most folks play. If you're really good, you play a one up–one back position because that player alone in the back is talented enough to play the entire court.

The receiver of the serve is also the spiker. The reception of the serve is so important in twos and in any Wallyball game. You're not going to get a good set to spike unless you make a good pass to the setter.

Twos is a good game for dinks and shallow shots off the side wall. Players often position themselves deep for slams and aren't able to play the short shot. It's also a good game in which to cross the defense up and hit the second shot over.

Twos Defense

The defense is as naked as the offense. Nothing fancy for you to do, and not a great deal of strategy to employ.

If the other team is passing exceptionally well and spiking winners close to the net, you might switch to a one up–one back, with the one up acting as a blocker. The defense cannot permit a spiker to slam without someone in his or her face.

Twos is a game where the offense can dominate quickly. On the defensive end, you really have to keep the offense guessing about what you're going to do. Give them a two-deep look and then slide someone to the net. Play a one-one and then drop the net player back. Fake a charge and stay two deep. If you can get them thinking about where you're going to be, instead of where they're going to hit the ball, you're going to be a winner.

8

DRILLS

We're loose, gang. Like rubberbands in sneakers and shorts. Now, we're really going to whomp that ball around. But before you show off your Wallyball skills to those awestruck friends, take a look around. Is the net up? Is it 8 feet high? Did someone remember to bring the ball?

Don't laugh. It's like the college football team rushing from the locker room after the coach has fired them up with a halftime speech only to discover that the door is locked. Wallyball is a simple game, but you can't play without a net and a ball, even if you are loose as a goose.

Before the game and after my stretching exercises, I try to take about 10 minutes to practice. Some people need more than 10 minutes; some need less. Take the time you need.

In the same way that basketball players have lay-up drills and shoot it around or that baseball infielders play pepper, Wallyballers have their pregame rituals. We may be new, but we have our traditions.

WALLYBALL PEPPER

Practice before a game should be fun, but it also should get you ready to play. And it's a good time to practice specific skills like serving, bump passing, or digging a ball off the wall.

Wallyball pepper. This practice drill can help all areas of your game: passing, setting, and spiking.

Probably the most common pregame drill is the Wallyball version of pepper. It's simple and fun, and you can do it with 2 players or 20 players. Let's say you have 4 on your team.

Just get yourselves in a little circle on one side of the net and start passing to one another. Start out standing just a few feet apart. You can bump-pass or set. Giggles and goofing around a little are allowed, but what you're doing is actually serious—getting a feel for the ball and practicing your passing. Watch your form. Are your hands held correctly? Are your arms together on the bump? Are they flat?

You ought to know that, when you are bumping, the ball strikes the forearms, not the hands. The forearms are stretched out, facing the ceiling and tightly parallel to each other. The hands are clasped.

If you want, you can gradually start moving farther away from each other on this drill, but don't do that too quickly. Bumping and setting accurately is tougher than it looks. It's OK to spend the entire time just doing short passes. Feel confident with those shorties before you even think about stretching them out.

HITTING AND PASSING

Another drill, sometimes done after pepper if you have the time, is a hitting and passing drill. You need at least 4 players for this and can do it with 6 or 8.

Divide up evenly on both sides of the net, with 1 player—the setter—at the net for each team. Have the other players play back as diggers and spikers. One of the players in the back passes to the setter, who does what setters are supposed to do: he or she sets. Either the digger or one of the other players comes up to spike. And he or she spikes to a player on the opposite side of the net, who attempts to pass the spike to the setter. Then the whole thing begins again.

SERVING AND DIGGING

Another team drill is for serving and digging. Teams are on their own side of the net. Start serving, back and forth. You should be intent on control and accuracy and move around, serving from different spots behind the service line. If you're unhittable hitting

Serving and digging. Don't try to annihilate your drill partner; just keep the ball in play and get into a rhythm.

the left wall from the right corner, try it the other way around. Then you'll be twice as tough.

While one team is serving, the other team can practice its reception of the serve by digging the practice serve as if it were the real thing. This serving and digging drill can be done with one or two balls.

TWO-BALL DRILL

If you do have two balls, here's a two-ball drill. Get a buddy and use only half of the court. One of you stands at the net with both Wallyballs. The other player stands in the middle of the court, facing

Two-ball drill. Improves speed and concentration.

the net. The net player tosses a ball against the side wall. The second player, using a forearm pass, passes it back to the net man.

Simple, so far. But remember that this is a two-ball drill. As soon as the second player's forearms strike the ball, a second ball is tossed against the other side wall. It is returned with another forearm pass, and another ball is launched.

This is all done quickly and tests the reflexes and quickness of the players as well as their passing skills. The net player does nothing but toss the ball against the side wall. After 20 or so hits, the players switch positions.

ONE-PERSON DRILLS

Sometimes, you want to play, but there's no one to Wally with. Sometimes, you just want to practice, but nobody's around. Here are a couple of drills you can do all by yourself.

Serving Accuracy

The first is a serving accuracy drill. A good server is the only player who can really dominate in Wallyball, and the good ones practice and practice. As you will see, there are lots of ways for the server to hit the ball, different spins to use, and lots of places for the ball to land.

One of the best places to hit that serve is deep and low on either side wall. *Deep* means about three-quarters deep along the wall. *Low* means waist-high or lower. Knee-high is even better. And if you can serve ankle-high, the other team probably shouldn't show up.

This drill is like shooting 50 free throws in basketball or target practice in archery. Get an 8-by-11-inch sheet of colored paper and tape it to the magic spot on the wall, let's say waist-high and three-quarters of the way down.

If you have taped it to the right side wall, serve from your left. Now, with good form, throw the ball over the net and try to hit your target. That's right, throw it. Do not hit it. You'll find it difficult at first, but it will become easier. What is difficult is chasing down every ball you throw.

After you have hit the mark 10 times in a row, then you may actually serve it. It's difficult, but keep at it. It may take a number of practice sessions to hit that piece of paper on a serve. I know some Wallyball fanatics who can serve and hit the paper 10 times and then move the paper to the other side wall and do it all over again.

Off the Wall

One last all-by-yourself practice, and then that's it. When I was a kid, I was a baseball nut and not a bad catcher. I remember throwing pop-ups to myself for hours. I know tennis players who practice their strokes against a wall.

The Wallyball equivalent of that is just to bump the ball against the wall. Play it off the wall and then bump it again. Bump it high; bump it low. Skin the wall with one hit; make it ricochet five feet on another shot. Set it, bump it, and set it again. It can be an easy drill or a hard one, depending on your skill and your stamina.

Practice drills aren't as fun as playing the game—that's obvious, but drills can help you to perfect your Wallyball skills so that once you're out on the court in a real game you can have longer volleys, set up spikes more frequently, and play a more competitive, more enjoyable game.

9
COED PLAY

I really have no way of knowing who's out there playing Wallyball. Racquetball club managers tell me that it isn't racquetball players. What they have told me, and what I have observed, is that the Wallyballer is often a team sport player, a softball player, a volleyball player, or someone who plays a Sunday game of two-hand touch.

The Wallyballer seems to like the social aspects of the sport as much as the sport itself. The player likes the workout during the game and the blowout afterwards.

And it seems that more and more women are playing the game.

I shouldn't be surprised at that because it is estimated that 60 percent of the 22 million recreational volleyball players in the United States—13.2 million—are women. On the high school level, the number of girls playing volleyball is 20 times higher than the number of boys.

Women have told me they like the game for lots of reasons: fun, a good sweat, the walls making every shot a possible winner, and the feeling that there really is no difference on the court between men and women.

In fact, there is only one difference between the men's and women's game of Wallyball—the net height. For the men's game, it is 8 feet. For the women, it is 7 feet, 4¼ inches.

Otherwise, it is the same game, and I've seen women dominate other women as well as men. They have had more spin on their serves than Martina Navratilova and have been bigger hitters than golfer Nancy Lopez.

In mixed men's and women's play, the net height is at eight feet. I've made one rule alteration to make sure that the two or three men playing with one woman don't freeze her out. In coed play, if there is more than a single hit, then the woman must make at least one hit on each point.

In our league play, a four-person coed team must have two men and two women. For those teams, the two-two alignment means a man and a woman up and a man and a woman back. Also, the serve must rotate between the sexes.

All of our league and tournament play—Novice, Intermediate, Advanced, and Open—is open to male, female, and mixed teams.

10
OTHER GAMES

I get buzzed (that's a California word that means "feeling good") when I see people enjoying themselves playing Wallyball. It makes me feel like I'm responsible for their good feeling.

I get even more buzzed when I see disabled people or senior citizens playing Wallyball. Or little kids. There are a number of variations to the game—some serious, some just for fun.

DISABLED

Some young men and women in wheelchairs have been playing the game and having a great time. It's a good exercise, stresses mobility, and promotes teamwork.

The four-wall court is a good teaching station because it lacks distractions and there are no worries about weather. Retrieving the ball is easy. Also, because the court is half the size of a volleyball court, it's simply easier for players in wheelchairs or with any other disability to get the ball over the net. One other point: Many racquetball clubs are on the ground floor, so there is wheelchair access.

Mixed group play is also not difficult in Wallyball. Combining wheelchair-bound and able-bodied people on the same team, or the developmentally disabled and others, makes Wallyball a great mainstreaming activity.

The rules can be changed in many ways, depending on the skills of the players. The game can be played with one or two bounces. The net could be lowered to six feet. A lighter ball, even a balloon, could be substituted for the Wallyball. And any kind of hit could be allowed.

We have discovered, through trial and error, that fours is too crowded for wheelchair athletes. Twos and threes seem to work more smoothly. For other disabilities, however, five or six could play on the same team.

KIDS

For kids, one bounce is OK. For littler kids, allow two bounces. We also lower the net and use a beach ball or another bouncier, lighter ball.

OLDER FOLKS

I've played with some older folks who would have wrapped that Wallyball around my Spanish eyes if I had even suggested giving them a break. But a bounce can be added, and the ball can be lighter.

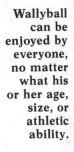

Wallyball can be enjoyed by everyone, no matter what his or her age, size, or athletic ability.

ONE ON ONE

Look, sometimes there's just you and a friend, and you can't find anyone else to play. And you *need* to play Wallyball.

Well, we do have a solution. It's called *one on one*, and it's played like this:

Each player gets two hits per shot and is permitted to hit it him- or herself. A serve cannot be hit against a side wall.

That's it. Otherwise, the rules are the same, and, if you lose, it's your shame.

WALLYBOO

There are a few silly Wallyball games, exercises in insanity that I often refer to as "drinking games." One is Wallyboo.

Wallyboo is the same as Wallyball, with one important addition: you put a sheet over the net.

With a sheet over the net, you cannot see the blue ball until it comes flying over the net. Every shot is a surprise, every return a wonder. Spikes are scary, and blocks are even scarier.

II

WALLYBALL RULES

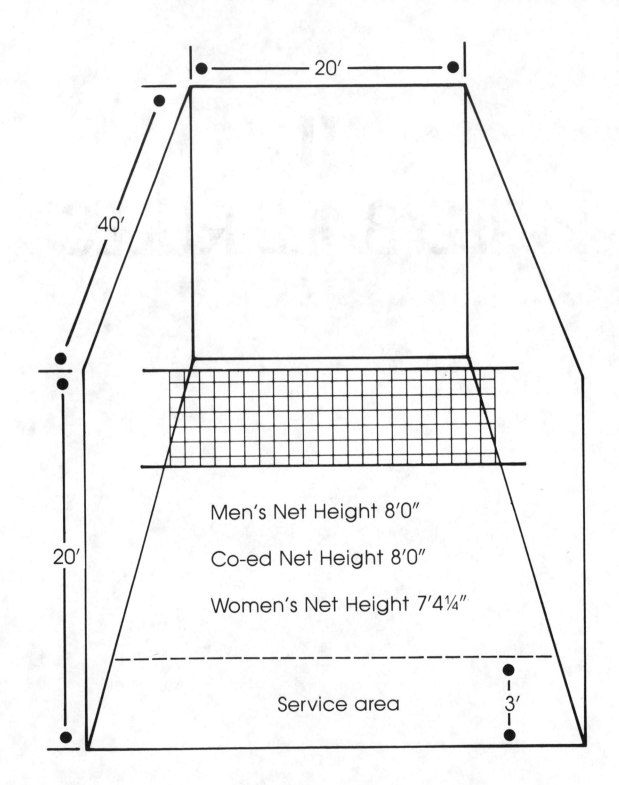

20'

40'

20'

Men's Net Height 8'0"

Co-ed Net Height 8'0"

Women's Net Height 7'4¼"

Service area

3'

1.00
COURT AREA AND EQUIPMENT

1.01 Court Area

The court area shall be 40 feet (12.1920 m) long by 20 feet (6.0960 m) wide by 20 feet (6.0960 m) high, the size of a standard racquetball court.

1.02 Net

The net shall be 3 feet wide overall and extend the entire width of the court. The net shall be installed across the center line of the court no higher than 8 feet (2.45 m) above the ground for men and no higher than 7 feet, 4¼ inches (2.24 m) above the ground for women. A check of the height and tension of the net shall be made before the start of each match and anytime the referee deems necessary. The height of the net should be checked at both ends of the net, perpendicular to the side boundary lines, as well as at the center of the net. After any adjustments have been made, the net should be tested so that a ball hitting the net rebounds properly.

1.03 Net Supports

Net supports shall be installed in the walls so as not to interfere with the playing of the game, the net, or the ball, or threaten the safety of the players.

1.04 The Ball

The ball shall be spherical, weighing not less than 250 grams (9 oz.) or more than 280 grams (10 oz.). The ball shall be not less than 25 inches (62 cm) or more than 27 inches (68 cm) in circumference. Ball pressure should not exceed 3 lbs.

1.05 Service Area

The service area is designated by a blue line 1½ inches wide, which extends the entire length of the court 3 feet from the back and front walls, respectively.

2.00
SCORING AND TIME-OUTS

2.01 Number of Games

All matches shall consist of the best two out of three games.

2.02 Point

A team, whether serving or on defense, receives a point·when the other team commits a fault.

2.03 Side-Out

A side-out (in the final four points of the game) is declared when the serving team commits a fault and the ball is turned over to the receiving team. No points can be scored on a side-out.

2.04 Match

A match is won by a team that wins two out of the three games.

2.05 Game

A game is won by the first team to score 21 points, provided there is a 2-point advantage. Both the serving and nonserving teams can score points. But the 19th, 20th, and 21st points and any points beyond can be scored only by the serving team.

2.06 Scoring in a Forfeited Game

If a game is forfeited due to an insufficient number of players or a team refusing to start a game, the forfeiting team shall lose the game by a score of 21–0. The forfeiting team shall lose the match by a score of 3–0.

2.07 Scoring in a Defaulted Game

If a team defaults due to the injury of a player or the dismissal of a team member by a referee, any points scored prior shall count. The winning team shall be awarded 21 points or at least enough points to allow them a 2-point advantage.

2.08 Requests for Time-Outs

A request for a time-out may be called only by the team captain when the ball is dead. A time-out may not be called once the score has been acknowledged.

2.09 Number of Time-Outs

Each team shall be allowed two (2) time-out periods limited to 30 seconds each per game. A team may terminate a time-out period before 30 seconds has expired by indicating they are ready to resume the game.

2.10 Failure to Return to Game after Time-Out Expires

If a team does not resume play immediately after the signal ending a time-out period, the team will be charged with another time-out. If both time-outs have been used by a team, the team shall be penalized and a point or side-out called, depending on which team has possession of the ball.

2.11 Consecutive Time-Outs

Two time-outs may be called consecutively by a team without resuming play. If a third time-out is called, a side-out or point will be awarded. If, however, the serving team calls a time-out in an attempt to disrupt play or gain an advantage, they shall be penalized with a loss of service. If a similar attempt for a third time-out is made by the receiving team, the serving team shall be awarded the point.

2.12 Injury Time-Out

The referee shall stop the game as soon as he discovers a player has been injured. If the injured player cannot continue the game, a substitution may be called, the game may be forfeited, or the team may play without the injured player—i.e., two against three, three against four. Up to two substitutions per game shall be allowed. A player cannot reenter a game in which he was injured; however, he may reenter a subsequent game of the match. An injury time-out of up to five (5) minutes may be granted the team with the injured player by the referee. A regular time-out period may be requested after an injury time-out has expired if the team has not used their two time-outs. If the game must be stopped or delayed to remove an injured player from the court, no time-out will be called no matter how long it takes to remove the player safely.

2.13 Time-Outs between Games

See Rule 3.07

3.00
RULES OF PLAY

3.01 Pre-Game Toss

A coin toss shall be made before the start of the first game of a match by the referee between the two team captains.

3.02 Pre-Game Warm-Ups

Warm-up periods of three (3) minutes will be allotted each team, either on the playing court or at another designated site to be determined by the referee. If both teams warm up on the playing court, the referee will allow six (6) minutes for the warm-ups. At then end of the warm-up period the referee shall sound his whistle to indicate play to begin. Once lineups are verified, no changes can be made. Any corrections made by players due to error in preparing their lineup sheets shall be refused.

3.03 Start of the Game

The referee shall call the score and direct play to begin.

3.04 Choice of Court Side or Service

The referee shall toss a coin between the teams' captains for choice of side or service. The winner of the coin toss shall choose to serve first or which side of the court his team shall play on during the first game of the match. The loser of the coin toss chooses the remaining option. The team not serving first in the first game shall serve first in the second game.

3.05 Choice of Court Side or Service in a Deciding Game

The team with the most total points (the total points scored in Games 1 and 2) shall choose the playing side or first serve in a deciding game. In the case of a tie, a retoss shall be required. Both teams shall change sides after one team scores 8 (15-point games) or 11 (21-point games) points in the deciding game. Service shall continue with the same server, and all other team members shall resume the same positions they were in before the change of sides took place.

3.06 Change of Playing Areas between Games

Except for a deciding game, teams and team players will change sides after each game of a match.

3.07 Time between Games

Changing playing areas and substitutions shall take place between games and should be made with a minimum of delay. Two (2) minutes shall be allotted between the first and second games of a match. Between the second and third games, five (5) minutes will be allotted. No extra time shall be allotted for changing sides.

3.08 Interruptions of Play

Play shall stop immediately in the event of an injury or when an object thrown on the playing court endangers a player's safety. When an interruption occurs, the point shall be replayed.

3.09 Match Interruptions

If a match cannot be finished due to insufficient time or equipment failure, the following shall apply:

1. If the game can be resumed at a later time on the same court, any points scored before the interruption shall count and the teams shall continue the game under the same conditions as before the interruption.
2. Any completed games of a match shall count.
3. If the game transfers to another playing area and continues or is cancelled and continued at a later date, any conditions that existed before the interruption shall apply.

3.10 Delaying the Game

Delaying the game unnecessarily for any reason whatsoever is grounds for a penalty if judged so by the referee. If a rest period has expired and a team has not reported back to the playing area, a time-out will be called on the team at fault. Up to two time-outs may be called by the referee on a team delaying the start of a game. If both time-outs are used and the team still does not resume play, the referee may declare a fault on the offending team.

3.11 Out of Bounds

The ball shall be called out of bounds whenever it hits the ceiling or back wall on the opponent's side or two or more walls consecutively on a serve, volley, or block.

3.12 Back Wall in Play or in Bounds

The back wall is in play only on the side of the team that is returning the serve or volley, provided a player on that team touches the ball first.

3.13 Ceiling in Play or in Bounds*

The ceiling is in bounds only on the side of the team that is returning the serve or volley, provided a player on that team touches the ball first.

3.14 Hitting the Ball Out of the Court Area

Anytime the ball is hit outside the court area, i.e., into the spectator's gallery or an adjacent court on the first or second hit or volley, the ball shall be declared dead and the point replayed. No loss of point or serve will be called. However, if the ball is hit into the spectator's gallery on a third hit or volley, a point or side-out will be called. If the ball touches the opponent's ceiling before leaving the court area, the ball will be called out of bounds and a side-out declared (loss of point or serve).

4.00
PLAYERS AND TEAMS—MAKEUP AND POSITIONS

4.01 Uniforms

All players shall comply with the proper player attire as stated in the rule book. Players shall dress in shorts, jerseys (T-shirts), and shoes (sneakers) with rubber soles. Jogging and/or running shoes with black tread soles are not permitted. Shoes shall be required at all times. It is preferred that members of the same team dress in same or similar colors and that their outfits be similar in style. Headgear, such as jewelry or large hairpins, is not allowed. If it is necessary to stop the game to remove illegal headgear or equipment, a time-out will be called. Sweatbands worn on the head or wrists are legal. Any taping or injury wrapping should be checked by the referee. No

---

*Since all racquetball courts do not have solid ceilings that extend the entire 40-foot length of the court, the tournament director shall decide whether the ceiling can be legally considered within bounds, depending on the physical characteristics of the court sponsoring the match.

hard casts of any kind are allowed! Soft casts may be allowed at the discretion of the referee.

4.02 Team Composition and Substitutions

The tournament director shall be given a roster of all team players, the team captain, and any substitutes before the start of each match. Any players not listed on the roster before a match shall not be allowed to play.

4.03 Number of Players

Each team shall be comprised of 2, 3, or 4 persons. Each team shall be allowed 2 substitutes or alternate players. When a team has been reduced to fewer than the allotted number of players, a substitution may be called, the game may be forfeited, or the game may continue with remaining players, i.e., 2 against 3, 3 against 4 (must continue to play by 4-person rule, 4.06).

4.04 Player Divisions

Teams entered in league or tournament play shall be classified into one of the following categories:

Open, Advanced, Intermediate, and Novice
Men's 2-, 3-, or 4-person teams
Women's 2-, 3-, or 4-person teams
Mixed 2-, 3-, or 4-person teams (on 4-person teams, 2 males and 2 females)
Open and Advanced divisions are limited to 2- and 3-person teams.

When a team wins a sanctioned tournament in a division, they must move to the next higher division in the next tournament season. The tournament director reserves the right to reclassify a team.

4.05 Substitutions

A position of a substitute shall be that of the player replaced without change in service order. Two substitutions per game are permitted. Only in case of injury can a player make a third entry or substitute in a different position. A substitution may be made only when the ball is dead and upon request of the playing captain. Once the referee acknowledges a substitution, the substitute is required to report in proper uniform and stand ready to enter the court when directed by the referee. A new substitution may not take place until play has resumed and the ball becomes dead or another time-out is called.

4.06 4-Person Rule

In 4-person play, the server on offense or defense *cannot spike or block.*

5.00
OFFICIALS—RESPONSIBILITIES AND POSITIONS

5.01 Referee's Power

The referee shall be in full charge of a match. The referee shall have the power to decide on any matters or questions not specifically covered in these rules and regulations, and his decision shall be final.

5.02 Referee and His Duties

The referee shall decide when the ball is in play or is dead and when a point has been made, and shall keep score. During interruptions in play, the referee shall be responsible for the ball. It shall be the responsibility of the referee to signal service at the beginning of each play, to interrupt play when a fault has been committed, and to request assistance from the tournament director or Wallyball regional representative when necessary.

5.03 Referee and His Position during Play

Referees shall position themselves in the viewing gallery directly above the playing court or in such a manner that they have an unobstructed view of the playing area. On courts with glass back walls and no viewing gallery, the referee shall be positioned directly behind the glass. On courts with glass side walls, the referee shall be positioned at the net. On courts that do not allow for some type of verbal communication between the referee and the playing teams, either a microphone or hand signals shall be used when calling plays during a game.

5.04 Referee and Keeping Time

The referee shall keep the official time during all time-out periods and rest periods between games of a match. The referee shall keep a record of the number of time-out periods each team has taken, and after each time-out period, the referee shall advise the coach or team captain as to the number of time-out periods remaining.

5.05 Referee and Player Positions

The referee shall make certain at the start of each game that the player positions on both teams correspond with the serving order listed on the scorecard.

5.06 Referee and Penalties

The referee shall decide matters of conduct concerning the behavior of coaches and players. The referee shall be the only official with the power to warn or penalize a team or one of its members. Any protests regarding penalties issued to players as a result of unsportsmanlike conduct shall not be reconsidered by the referee. If requested from a team captain, the referee must give his reason for issuing a penalty; however, the decision of the referee shall stand. (See 5.09.)

5.07 Tournament Director

It is the responsibility of the tournament director to secure a sanctioned Wallyball referee for the tournament.

5.08 Playing Captain

One playing team member shall be designated as the playing captain and shall have his name listed on the scorecard before the start of the game. If the playing captain leaves a game, a new playing captain shall be designated to assume the duties of captain for the remainder of the game or until the designated captain returns.

5.09 Protesting an Officials Decision

Only the playing captain may protest the decision of a referee if he addresses the referee prior to the first service following the play in which the disagreement occurred. If the team captain cannot resolve a difference with a referee, the referee's decision shall stand; however, the team captain has the power to take the protest to the tournament director.

6.00
THE SERVICE

6.01 Legal Service

The player in the back position of the court shall put the ball in play by hitting it with one hand only or any part of his arm in an attempt to send the ball over the net and into the opponent's court. The serve is good if the ball passes over the net without touching a member of the serving team or the net. A served ball that hits a wall on either the serving team's side or the receiving side is good, provided the ball contacted only one wall before landing in the opponent's court.

6.02 Preliminary Service Action

Bouncing or lightly tossing the ball prior to executing the serve is legal. The server has five (5) seconds after the referee sounds his whistle to release the ball and execute the serve. Once the ball is tossed in the air, the ball shall be struck for service unless the server catches the ball before making contact with it. If the server catches a ball, the serve shall be canceled and replayed. Guiding or directing or pushing the serve is illegal. A serve must be cleanly struck.

6.03 Serving before the Referee Calls the Score

A serve that is attempted before the referee calls the score shall be canceled and replayed.

6.04 The Service Line

When the ball is hit for service, no part of the server's body can be in contact with the service line. The server may step onto or over the service line after the serve has been executed. The server's body may be entirely in the air over the service line at the moment of service as long as the last contact with his body and the floor were within the legal serving area.

6.05 Length of the Service

Service shall continue by a team until a fault is committed by the serving team and the ball turned over to the opponents (side-out) or the game is completed.

6.06 Illegal Position of the Server

The game shall stop immediately when the server has been discovered out of the designated serving order. Any points earned while the server was in an illegal position shall be canceled and a side-out declared. If the server is discovered out of the designated service order after a side-out is called, all points scored shall count. A verification of the service order may be requested from time to time by the team captains. It is the responsibility of the playing captain to tell the referee if there is a player serving out of order.

6.07 Service in Subsequent Games

Except for a deciding game, the team that did not receive the first service of the first game of the match shall serve first the next game of the match.

6.08 Serving Order

Players must maintain the serving order as listed in the official scorecard. Serving order may be changed after each game only. In 4-person play, the server cannot spike or block. The rule is in effect for the defense or offense.

6.09 Screening

No members of the serving team may block the server from the opposing team by raising their hands above their heads, flailing their arms from side to side, or forming groups of two or more to hide the actions of the server. Players on the serving team who deliberately switch their positions and block the server from the opposing team may be subject to penalty.

6.10 Player Positions at Service

All players, except the server, shall have both feet fully on the ground during the serve. In 4-person play, players must be in their designated serving *positions*. After the service, players may move to an alternate offensive or defensive position. In 2- and 3-person play, *only* the service order (rotation) must be maintained.

6.11 Receiving the Serve with an Open-Hand Pass

It is illegal for a player to receive a serve with an open-hand pass or to set the serve.

6.12 Service Faults

Any of the following committed during the service shall count as a fault:

1. A served ball contacts the net. (Refer to 7.01.)
2. A served ball lands in the next court or in the spectator's gallery. (Refer to 3.14.)
3. A serve is not executed from the designated service area. (Refer to 6.04.)
4. A server crosses the service line at the same time the serve is executed. (Refer to 6.04.)
5. A served ball hits a member on the serving team. (Refer to 6.01.)
6. A serve is delivered by the wrong server. (Refer to 6.06.)
7. The serve was executed improperly. (Refer to 6.01.)
8. Players on the serving team screen the server from the opposing team. (Refer to 6.09.)

7.00
PLAY AT THE NET

7.01 Touching the Net

A ball that touches or rebounds off the net or net hardware may be played again, provided it was not on the serve. If the ball is hit 3 times by a team but does not cross the net, the referee shall wait until a 4th contact is made or the ball hits the ground before stopping play.

7.02 Ball Crossing the Net

A ball that crosses over the net entirely is considered good.

7.03 Part of Ball Contacting and Crossing the Net

If only part of a ball crosses the net and is subsequently hit by an opponent, the ball is considered as having crossed the net.

7.04 Player Contact with the Net

A player or any part of his body or uniform that touches the net while the ball is in play shall be charged with a fault, unless the ball is driven into the net with such force that it causes the net to touch a player.

7.05 Reaching Over the Net

In returning the ball, a player may follow through over the net, provided he first makes contact with the ball on his side of the playing court. Players attempting a block may reach across the net but shall not contact the ball until an opponent strikes the ball in an attempt to send it back into the opponent's court. A player cannot block an opponent's set. If an opponent's set crosses the vertical plane of the net, it is considered a free ball, and both teams are entitled to it.

7.06 Recovering the Ball from the Net

A ball may be recovered and played from the net.

7.07 Crossing the Center Line

A player may not cross over the center line at any time. A player may step on, but cannot go over, the center line. If a player lands on the center line and interferes with an opponent, the referee shall declare a side-out or loss of service, depending on which team committed the fault.

7.08 Simultaneous Contact by Opponents

A double fault will be called and the point replayed when opposing players contact the net simultaneously.

7.09 Ball Crossing the Vertical Plane of the Net

A ball that crosses beneath the vertical plane of the net may be played or returned by an attacking team player, provided he does not interfere with an opponent.

7.10 Ball Directly Above the Vertical Plane of the Net

A ball directly above the vertical plane of the net may be played by either team.

7.11 Dead Ball

A ball becomes dead when:

1. The ball hits the floor.
2. The ball hits two or more walls consecutively on the receiving team's side. (Refer to 8.06.)
3. The ball hits the ceiling on the opponent's side. (Refer to 3.13.)
4. The ball hits the back wall on the fly on the receiving team's side. (Refer to 3.11.)
5. The ball is hit out of the court and into the viewing gallery. (Refer to 3.14.)
6. A served ball hits the net. (Refer to 7.01.)
7. The referee sounds his whistle. (Refer to 6.03.)
8. A player commits a fault. (Refer to 9.04.)

7.12 The Honor Call

All players shall call out loud when they hit or touch the net.

7.13 Ball Passing Through Net Opening

Since some nets may not extend the full width of the court, any ball passing through the net opening on the first or second hit of a volley will be *replayed*. A ball passing through the net opening on the third hit or serve will be a side-out or point.

8.00
PLAYING THE BALL

8.01 Number of Contacts with the Ball

Up to three (3) successive contacts with the ball are allowed each team in order to play the ball over the net and into an opponent's court. Contacting the wall does not count as a set or play.

8.02 Contacted Ball

Any player that makes contact with the ball shall be considered as having played the ball.

8.03 Successive Contact with the Ball by a Player

A player shall not make successive contacts with the ball except when playing a hard-driven spiked ball. Successive contact with a spiked ball shall count as one attempt to play the ball.

8.04 Simultaneous Contact with the Ball by Blockers

A player who participates in a block and makes only one attempt to play the ball during the block may make successive contact with the ball during such play even though it is not a hard-driven spike ball. Players participating in a block may participate in the next play; this second contact shall count as the first of three hits allowed a team.

8.05 Simultaneous Body Contact with the Ball

Any part of the body including or above the waist can hit the ball simultaneously so long as the ball rebounds quickly after such contact.

8.06 Playing 2 or More Walls

Contacting 2 or more walls with the ball is allowed only by the team in possession of the ball on their own side, provided a player on that team touches the ball first. If the ball crosses the net after contacting two or more walls without making contact with a player, a side-out or loss of serve will be called.

8.07 Consecutive Contact

Each contact with the ball shall be made by a different member of the same team. If consecutive hits are made by the same player, a fault will be declared.

8.08 Mishandling the Ball

Holding, lifting, scooping, pushing, or carrying the ball with 1 or 2 open hands—either underhand or overhand—is a fault, and a side-out or loss of serve will be called.

8.09 Simultaneous Holding by Opponents

A double fault shall be called and the point replayed when players from opposing teams simultaneously hold the ball. If holding is not called, play shall continue. Whichever side of the net the ball falls on after simultaneous holding, that team shall be allowed up to 3 contacts with the ball.

8.10 Simultaneous Contact by Teammates

If two players on the same team hit the ball simultaneously, one contact with the ball will be called, and either player may contact the ball on the next play.

8.11 Team Assistance

Teammates shall not hold or assist one another while making a play.

8.12 Blocking

Any player may raise his hands above his shoulders close to the net and attempt to intercept the ball from an opponent. A block does not count as one of the 3 successive contacts allowed a team and may be attempted before the ball passes over the net, while the ball is still in the opponent's court or just as the ball crosses the net. A block is good only if the ball is touched by the player attempting the block. A blocked ball counts as having crossed over the net. A team may attempt a block if (a) a player on the attacking team serves or spikes the ball; (b) the opponents have made 3 contacts on the ball; or (c) the ball falls near the net but no player on the attacking team can reasonably make a play on the ball.

8.13 Climbing the Wall to Block

Climbing the wall to block or set or serve is illegal.

8.14 Multiple Contacts with the Ball During a Block

Multiple contacts with the ball between players participating in a block is legal. A player who participates in a block may contact the ball on the next play, since blocking is not considered one of the 3 hits allowed a team.

8.15 Deflecting the Ball off the Back Wall

If a player contacts the ball in such a manner that the ball deflects off the back wall on his side of the court and goes over the net, the ball shall be considered good.

8.16 Spiking the Ball

Any player may spike the ball in 2- or 3-person team play.

8.17 Ball Spinning into Opponent's Court and Returning

A ball that spins off the net into an opponent's court and subsequently returns to the team originally in possession of the ball shall be good, provided it occurred on the first or second contact by the team. If the ball spins off the net on the third hit allowed a team, a side-out will be called. Any team member other than the last player to hit the ball can participate in the second or third hit after a ball returns from spinning into an opponent's court.

8.18 Dinks

Players cannot dink the ball with an open hand. They must use a closed fist, knuckles, or cobra shot.

9.00
TEAM AND PLAYER FAULTS COMMITTED DURING PLAY

9.01 Double Fault

When two opposing players commit faults simultaneously, a double fault shall be called and the point replayed.

9.02 Opponents Committing Faults at the Same Time

When opposing players commit faults at approximately the same time, the team that committed the fault first shall be penalized. If the referee cannot decide which team committed the fault first, a double fault will be declared.

9.03 Penalty for a Fault

A fault called on the serving team will result in a side-out or point, and the ball will be turned over to the receiving team. If the receiving team commits a fault, the serving team shall score a point.

9.04 During-Play Faults

Any of the following committed during play by a player or a team shall count as a fault:

1. The ball is played more than 3 times consecutively by a team. (Refer to 8.01.)
2. The ball touches the ceiling on the opponent's side. (Refer to 3.13.)
3. The ball hits 2 or more walls consecutively on the receiving team's side. (Refer to 8.06.)
4. The ball hits the back wall on a fly or volley on the receiving team's side. (Refer to 3.11.)
5. The ball hits the floor of the court.
6. The ball is hit twice by the same player consecutively. (Refer to 8.07.)
7. The net is touched by a player while the ball is in play. (Refer to 7.07.)
8. A player crosses the center line and touches an opponent. (Refer to 7.04.)
9. The ball contacts a player below the waist. (Refer to 8.05.)
10. A player holds the ball. (Refer to 8.08.)
11. The ball is thrown or pushed by a player. (Refer to 8.08.)
12. The ball lands outside the court or in the spectator's gallery. (Refer to 3.14.)
13. A personal penalty is called on a player. (Refer to 11.03.)
14. A game is delayed. (Refer to 2.10.)
15. A substitution is made illegally. (Refer to 4.05.)
16. An illegal block is attempted. (Refer to 8.14.)
17. Players purposely distract the opponents. (Refer to 11.02[5].)
18. A time-out exceeds 30 seconds. (Refer to 2.10.)
19. A player illegally assists a teammate. (Refer to 8.11.)

10.00
MISCELLANEOUS

10.01 Coed Play

The rules involving males and females on the same team shall be the same as the rules that govern all team players except for the following:

1. Men and women shall alternate service within a team on the court in 2- or 4-person play.
2. A female team member shall make one contact with the ball if the ball is played more than once by a team.
3. A block does not count as one of the three contacts allowed a team. If the ball is blocked by a male player, another male player may hit the ball back into the opponent's court.

10.02 Responsibility for Securing a Referee

It is the responsibility of the tournament director to secure a sanctioned Wallyball referee for tournament play. In league play, it is the responsibility of the home team to supply a referee.

10.03 Wearing Protective Equipment Due to Injury

Any injured player required to wear protective padding or supportive equipment due to injury shall not automatically be excluded from play. At the discretion of the referee, the safety and potential hazards to other players shall be examined and the final decision made by the referee.

11.00
CONDUCT AND SANCTIONS

11.01 Team Conduct

All players and coaches shall be apprised of all rules and regulations concerning Wallyball and observe them at all times. The team captain shall be responsible for the conduct and behavior of his team. The team captain shall be considered spokesperson for his team and the only player allowed to address the referee. Any other player speaking directly to a referee shall be warned and may be penalized.

11.02 Improper Conduct Subject to Penalty

Any and all of the following acts committed by the team players are subject to penalty:

1. Continuous disagreement with officials concerning their decisions.
2. Use of vulgar or profane language toward officials, opponents, or spectators.
3. Disruptive comments or noises during a game from outside the court.
4. Use of actions intended to influence the decisions of officials.
5. Moving or crossing the vertical plane of the net with any part of the body to distract an opponent while the ball is in play.
6. Yelling or other loud noises made to distract an opponent playing or attempting to play a ball.
7. Leaving the court during a break in the game without the express permission of the referee.
8. Unnecessary clapping of hands by teammates at the moment

contact is made with the ball by a player, especially during the serve.

9. Unnecessary shouting or any activity that may distract the referee from rendering proper judgment regarding the handling of the ball.
10. Kicking or throwing the ball in an abrupt manner, whether during play or between games.

11.03 Sanctions

Violations committed by coaches, players, and/or team members may result in the following sanctions:

1. *Warning*—A warning will be issued for minor offenses, e.g., causing a delay in the game or talking with opponents, spectators, or officials. A warning will be recorded on the score sheet. If a second warning is given, a penalty will result.
2. *Penalty*—A second minor offense or rude conduct will result in a penalty. A penalty is recorded on the scoresheet and will automatically cause the loss of the serve, if the penalty was called on the serving team. If the penalty was called on the receiving team, a point will be awarded. Two penalties issued by the referee will result in expulsion of a player.
3. *Expulsion*—Obnoxious or unruly behavior, such as profane or vulgar language toward officials, spectators, or opponents, will result in the expulsion of a player from the game. Two expulsions during a match by the referee shall result in the disqualification of a player or team member for the remainder of the tournament.
4. *Disqualification*—Any act of physical aggression, attempted or actuated toward an official, spectator, or opponent, will result in the immediate disqualification of a player or team member for the remainder of the tournament. Disqualified players shall be required to leave the game area, including the viewing area.

RULING SITUATIONS

1.02 Court Area and Equipment

Situation: The referee and visiting mixed-doubles teams arrive at the match and discover a sagging net that is less than 8 feet above the floor.
Ruling: The match shall be conducted.
Comment: Every effort should be made by the host team to make the sagging net legal, but neither the visiting team nor the referee may cancel the match.

Situation: Team A, on its second play, hits the ball between the side wall and the edge of the net.
Ruling: Replay is called.
Comment: On the first or second hit, a replay is called by the referee; on the third hit, a side-out or point is awarded to Team B.

2.05 Game Point

Situation: Team A has just served their 20th point, with the score resulting in Team A, 20, Team B, 19.
Ruling: Team A must score 1 more point to be declared winner of the game.
Comment: Teams shall continue to play until one team has a 2-point advantage.

2.08 Time-Outs

Situation: During a volley a player from Team B (a) loses a contact lens; (b) breaks a knee brace; (c) hits a ball that shatters a light fixture over Team B's playing court.
Ruling: In (a), (b), and (c) the referee will call for a time-out to make repairs. This would not be charged to either team.
Comment: After repairs and corrections are made, the referee shall declare a replay.

2.10–2.11 Consecutive Time-Outs

Situation: Team A requires a 60-second time-out to go over a defensive move.
Ruling: Legal. Team A is then charged with 2 time-out periods.
Comment: If Team A was already charged with a time-out during that game, then point or side-out is awarded Team B with play to begin immediately.

2.12 Injury Time-Out

Situation: A player on Team B injures her ankle, and the referee interrupts play. Team B's player is ready to play (a) within 5 minutes; (b) after 5 minutes.
Ruling: (a) and (b) are both legal. (a) No time-out is charged; (b) a time-out is charged Team B.
Comment: If the coach realizes the player will not be able to play within the 5-minute time allotment, he must substitute to avoid the charged time-out.

3.02 Rules of Play

Situation: Team A discovers an error in their service order after the

lineups have been verified by the referee but before the start of the game.
Ruling: Illegal. No changes can be made once the lineups are officially verified.

3.05 Choice of Court Side or Service in a Deciding Game

Situation: Team A has a total of 36 points in 2 games, and Team B has 38 points. Team B chooses to serve first.
Ruling: Legal. Team A has choice of side of court.
Comment: In the case of a tie, a retoss shall be required.

3.08 Interruptions in Play

Situation: A substitute player from Team A accidentally drops a knee pad down onto the playing court from the viewing area above during a very important play.
Ruling: Replay.
Comment: Play shall stop immediately and the object shall be removed from court; therefore, no apparent danger to players.

3.07 & 3.10 Time between Games and Delaying the Game

Situation: Following the first game, Team A returns to the floor and is ready to play after 30 seconds have elapsed. Team B is not in position to play until (a) 1 minute has expired; (b) 2 minutes have expired; (c) 2 minutes and 5 seconds have expired.
Ruling: (a) and (b) are legal, but (c) is unnecessary delay by Team B.
Comment: If both teams are ready, the referee may begin play before 2 minutes have elapsed between games. In situation (c) a time-out is assessed Team B with only one time-out remaining during that game.

3.13 Ceiling in Play or in Bounds

Situation: Team A, on its second play, hits the ball into the ceiling; a player on Team A is able to recover the ball and at the same time send the ball over the net.
Ruling: Legal.
Comment: The ceiling is in bounds only on the side of the team that hit the ball into the ceiling.

3.14 Hitting the Ball Out of the Court Area

Situation: On its third hit, Team B sends the ball into the spectators' gallery.
Ruling: Point or side-out will be called.

Situation: On its second play, Team B hits the opponents' ceiling before leaving the court area.
Ruling: Point or side-out will be called.
Comment: The ball hitting the opponents' ceiling is an out-of-bounds call.

4.03 Number of Players

Situation: In mixed doubles, due to an injury, a team is forced to play with 1 woman and 2 men. During a play, the 2 men with 2 hits send the ball across the net.
Ruling: Illegal. Even though the team is forced to play with 1 woman, the 4-person mixed-doubles rules still pertain.

4.06 In 4-Person Play

Situation: Team B is serving. The player on Team B makes the first play; a teammate sets the ball, and the server spikes the ball over the net to the floor.
Ruling: Illegal. The server cannot block or spike the ball.

5.02 Referee and His Duties

Situation: After Team A scores a point, it is brought to the attention of the referee, by the captain of Team B that during a rally, a player from Team A touched the net during an attempted block.
Ruling: Even though this is illegal, the foul was not seen by the referee, so no penalty shall be assessed. The point stands.

Situation: The referee notices that the captain of Team B requests to have the serving order checked several times during the game.
Ruling: Legal. It is the captain's right to check serving order.
Comment: The referee may refuse on the basis he or she thinks Team B is doing this to interfere with the momentum of Team A, or that Team B is using this as an additional time-out to plan game strategy.

6.02 Preliminary Service Action

Situation: The server is acknowledged with the score from the referee. The server tosses the ball and decides it is not a good toss. The server catches the ball, bounces it 2 times, and tosses the ball the second time prior to the serve.
Ruling: Legal, as long as the server executes the serve within 5 seconds.

6.03 Serving before the Referee Acknowledges the Game Score

Situation: Before the referee acknowledges the server with the

score, the ball is served.
Ruling: Referee cancels that serve, and the same person serves again after score has been repeated.
Comment: Server gets an additional 5 seconds for this serve.

6.09 Screening

Situation: Two players on Team A deliberately stand together in front of the server to screen his serve.
Ruling: Illegal. No members of the serving team may block the server from the opposing team.

7.04 Player Contact with the Net

Situation: In an attempt to block the ball, a Team B player's shoulder is hit with the net because of a net shot from Team A.
Ruling: Legal. The net contact with the player's body was due to a ball driven with such force that it caused the net to touch the player.

7.05 Reaching over the Net

Situation: A player on Team A reaches over the net to execute a block.
Ruling: Legal.
Comment: Players attempting to block may reach across the net but shall not contact the ball until an opponent strikes the ball in an attempt to send it back into the opponent's court.

7.09 Ball Crossing the Vertical Plane of the Net

Situation: Team A's second play has caused the ball to have passed partially under the net, when it is interfered with unintentionally by Team B. Team A is attempting to play the ball a third time.
Ruling: Illegal. Net foul is called, interference on Team B.

7.10 Ball Directly Above the Vertical Plane of the Net

Situation: On Team B's second hit a player sets the ball directly above the net, allowing Team A's player to spike the ball to the floor.
Ruling: Legal. A ball directly above the vertical plane of the net may be played by either team.

8.03 Successive Contact with the Ball by a Player

Situation: A player on Team A saves a spiked ball so it deflects off her hand to her biceps and shoulder.
Ruling: Legal. Successive contact is permitted when recovering a hard-driven spike.

Situation: A player on Team A spikes the ball. It is deflected by a player on Team B and saved by another player on Team B, who allows to ball to deflect from hand to shoulder.
Ruling: Illegal. Double hit is called.
Comment: Multiple contacts by the player in an attempt to save the spike are permitted only if it is the first play for that player's team.

8.04 Simultaneous Contact with the Ball by Blockers

Situation: Players A and B both go up for a block. The ball hits the hand of both players.
Ruling: Legal. This shall be considered a block, and the team shall be allowed three additional hits.

8.14 Multiple Contacts with the Ball During a Block

Situation: A player blocks a ball, then hits it again to a teammate, who sets it back to another teammate, who spikes the ball.
Ruling: Legal.

8.17 Ball Spinning into the Opponent's Court and Returning

Situation: Team A's player, on her second hit, sends the ball across the net, hitting the ball with such spin that it rebounds back to Team A's side of the net, with the teammate sending it back across the net again.
Ruling: Legal. The play was executed with three hits.

9.01 Double Fault

Situation: A player on Team A spikes the ball, but at the instant the ball hits the floor on Team B's side of the court, the spiker contacts the net.
Ruling: Double foul.
Comment: Team B's failure to return the ball is a foul, as is the net foul by the player. Because they occur at the same instant, the proper call is a double foul and a replay.

9.04 During-Play Faults

Situation: A player on Team A sets the serve to a teammate, who then spikes the ball across the net.
Ruling: Illegal. A player cannot receive the serve with an open hand.

10.01 Coed Play

Situation: In the first game of a coed match, Team A loses a female'

player due to injury. There is no substitution.
Ruling: Team A is permitted to finish the match, but must still abide by the rules governing coed play.

11.02 Improper Conduct Subject to Penalty

Situation: Team A's player loudly stomps his feet and claps his hands during Team B's serve.
Ruling: A penalty is issued to Team A's player, and point is awarded to Team B.

GLOSSARY

Attacking—Hitting the ball into the opponent's court.

Attack block—An attempt to intercept the ball before it crosses the net.

Block—A play by one or more players who attempt to intercept the ball over or near the net.

Contacted ball—A ball that touches or is touched by any part of a player's body or clothing.

Dig—A pass of a spiked ball while standing, diving, rolling, or jumping.

Dink—Usually a one-hand hit in which the tips of the fingers are used to hit the ball to an area of the opponent's court.

Dive—At attempt to recover a ball by going to a prone position on the court.

Forearm pass—A ball played off the forearms in an underhanded manner.

Foul—A failure to play the ball properly, as permitted under the rules.

Netting—Touching the net while the ball is in play.

Off-speed shot—A ball that rapidly loses momentum due to a reduced speed of the striking arm just prior to contact.

Pass—The reception of the serve or first contact of the ball. It is an attempt to control the movement of the ball to another player.

Seam—The area directly between two receivers or diggers.

Serve overhand—A serve performed with an overhand throwing action. The ball is usually contacted with the heel of the hand.

Serve underhand—A serve performed with an underhand striking action. The ball is usually contacted with the heel of the hand.

Set—A pass that places the ball in position for a player to spike.

   Back set—A set made over the head behind the setter, executed with two hands.

   Jump set—The player setting the ball jumps to confuse the block or to place himself in a better position to save a long pass that will drop over or hit the net.

   One set—An extremely low vertical set delivered from one to two feet above the net. The spiker contacts the ball while the set is rising.

   Regular set—A ball that is delivered in a high arc that should drop about two feet from the net.

Setter—The player who sets the ball to the spiker.

Side-out—When the serving team fails to score a point, the ball is given to the opponents, and exchange of service is called a *side-out*.

Spike—A ball hit forcibly with one hand.

Spiker—A player who performs a spike, dink, or off-speed shot.

Thrown ball—The ball must be cleanly hit. When, in the opinion of the proper official, the ball visibly comes to rest at contact, the player shall have committed a foul.

Transition—Changing from offense to defense or vice versa.

INDEX